INNOVATION
VISION
COMMUNITY
SUSTAINABILITY
CONNECTION
SELF-SUFFICIENCY

THE PRINCE'S
COUNTRYSIDE
FUND

'It's clear to me that there are huge
opportunities to help the countryside
and rural people meet the challenges
of the future. But we do need to be clear
about what we want to achieve, thinking
particularly about what will be important
to our children and grandchildren.
The role of the countryside, with
all its diversity and idiosyncrasies,
in our national life is too important
to be left to chance.'

HRH The Prince of Wales

Writing as guest editor of Country Life
to celebrate his 70th birthday, November 2018

**THE PRINCE'S
COUNTRYSIDE
FUND**

The Prince's Countryside Fund,
137 Shepherdess Walk, London N1 7RQ
princescountrysidefund.org.uk

Registered charity no. England and Wales 1136077;
Scotland SC048055

Company limited by guarantee no. 07240359

Produced by Eye to Eye Media on behalf of The Prince's Countryside Fund.
Axe & Bottle Court, 70 Newcomen Street, London SE1 1YT.
Writers: Cathy Howes, Helen Aldis. Illustrator: Mark Long

CONTENTS

THE VILLAGE
SUSTAINABILITY
TOP 10

To meet the challenges facing rural communities, villages are coming together to create the services and assets they need, now and for generations to come. To help safeguard the future viability of villages, The Prince's Countryside Fund has come up with these ways for them to...

1 Create a village vision From a small idea or neighbourhood plan to a bigger, more ambitious project, you need a clear, strategic vision for your village. Identify your priorities, now and for the future, and the resources you need to make them viable in the long term.

2 Form a forum to come together Whether your group is a parish council or a committee focused on one task, include a range of people from all demographics in the community. Reach out to farmers, landowners and local businesses to identify – and respond to – your needs. Put together a plan and work with your local authority to find ways to make your ideas stronger and easier to deliver.

3 Give a voice to all A strong, thriving community is an inclusive one, so give residents of all ages and backgrounds time and space to collaborate and understand each other's needs.

4 Find a space to meet Every village needs a place to meet, talk and build a sense of community, whether that's a pub, shop, village hall or a post office in a church. Look after and maintain your assets to stop them being lost forever. Once gone, they're very difficult to replace.

5 Expand your connections
A rural community can't operate in isolation. You need good transport links and connections to the local market town, schools, hospitals and businesses if you're going to attract people to your village to live and work. Learning new skills and building people's confidence in digital communication and e-commerce is essential for future access to services.

6 Nurture a wider network Learn from the experiences of other communities, or ask for advice and support from local and national organisations to shape your plans. Bring in experienced experts or facilitators, or engage with local businesses to help get new community initiatives off the ground.

7 Develop self-sufficiency
Communities shouldn't be left to 'go it alone', but there are times when the best outcome is for a village to come together to solve its own problems. This could be through some form of community ownership, volunteer schemes, or support networks – face to face and digital.

8 Discover your creative spirit and take an innovative approach
Have the confidence to try something new. Take inspiration from others who've had a go and seek advice and help from a variety of support organisations. Solutions come in different forms, from libraries in pubs and community cafés, to transport apps, energy schemes and affordable housing projects.

9 Build financial resilience
Developing a diverse, thriving local economy will help your community remain sustainable in the future. Whether this is through improved access to training or support, better local employment opportunities, or by creating a place to do business – it all helps.

10 Become a strong community
A strong, resilient community is one that knows all the people within it, the skills they have and the services they need. It also has the drive to come together to support and deliver these services – in partnership with others or with the community as a whole.

THE
VILLAGE
SPIRIT

...is alive and well and rising to the challenges of rural living everywhere. And no one knows this better than Miranda Hart, comedy writer, actress and enthusiastic ambassador for The Prince's Countryside Fund. Miranda has lived in – and loved – the countryside her whole life, making her the ideal rural champion to introduce The Village Survival Guide

INTRODUCTION

by Miranda Hart

'I'm incredibly grateful to everyone from generations past and present who've had a hand in protecting and sustaining our land, so that I'm able to enjoy living in it and from it.'

I feel very honoured to have been asked to write an introduction to The Village Survival Guide. Honoured on three counts: my passion for the countryside; the importance of this practical, encouraging and supportive guide; and to be involved in a small way in The Prince's Countryside Fund in my new role of ambassador (if I see any of you in the country anytime soon I expect to be called Ambassador Hart and, ideally, be curtsied to!).

I assume most of you reading this share my passion for the countryside, our unique British landscape and keeping rural communities flourishing. Our individual reasons for that passion will vary from simply the love of being in nature, to animal welfare and protecting species, farming, village life and all the myriad joys the country brings. I'm incredibly grateful to everyone from generations past and present who've had a hand in protecting and sustaining our land, so that I'm able to enjoy living in it and from it.

I have lived rurally on and off throughout my life. I was born in Devon and although I only lived there for my first two years, family holidays always took us back. I believe those formative experiences instilled in me a love of remote landscapes such as Dartmoor and the wildlife, rivers, rock-pool swimming and the sea. Delights that remain great loves of mine.

I spent my childhood years in a Hampshire village near Petersfield, and it was in the vibrant village hall that I started my comedy career. If it wasn't for the villagers taking time outside of work and family commitments to maintain all aspects of that hall to keep it fit for productions, I can't imagine where I would have first been able to try out my writing and performing. And, more to the point, if it wasn't for the kindly friends, family and neighbours who supported the shows and, in most cases, probably pretended to laugh and encourage me – I cannot vouch for the quality of my first village hall productions! But they certainly did sow the seeds of many things that came later, so I owe much to that village infrastructure and the safe community it provided me generally. I was very fortunate to live somewhere with a regular bus service, access to good local doctors, and a community with the enthusiasm for the arts of every kind (my mother in her 80th year still plays piano for the choir). I know not all village life is as lucky.

Recognising rural challenges

Despite the beauty, mystery, wonder and importance of rural living, I am only too aware of some of the challenges. For the last six years I have predominantly lived in Sussex – there were spells of work that drove me back to the Big Smoke where I would feel like a trapped animal. (You know you are a very proud country bumpkin when returning to a city makes you feel permanently hot and cross – I often thought it was an early menopause before I realised it was simply concrete, people and traffic!)

Sussex is wonderful, but despite that – and however much my heart yearns for open wilderness over crowded cities – my patience was often tested. For example, sending a text message would mean hanging out of a window at a particularly athletic and unstable angle that wouldn't have passed any health and safety measures – and that I wasn't in any way agile enough for – just to get a mobile signal! Or when on a cold winter's evening after tirelessly getting in logs to keep the much-needed fire going, all I wanted was to curl up and watch a Netflix movie, yet I was denied that pleasure due to the limited broadband network and so was faced with that buffering wheel of doom on my laptop. I never felt it fair that the effective use of technology belonged on

COUNTRY BORN AND BRED
From a childhood in Hampshire (top), to the serenity of Sussex today, with loyal companion Peggy

solely to city dwellers, and I was keenly aware that any time I mentioned country living issues, those city dwellers wouldn't understand. It was as if they thought you shouldn't complain – the assumption being that you lived in a tranquil idyll without any of the stresses of urban living and therefore a permanent state of bliss. But after the local council told me they wouldn't be coming up to the end of the track to my cottage (it was fairly remote) to collect rubbish, and I was carrying two heavy, smelly bin bags down the lane to the nearby farm because it was too muddy to take my car down, it certainly did not feel remotely idyllic. And when I inevitably slipped and found myself face to face with a cowpat, far from blissful. I think people imagined healthy flushed cheeks, constant sunshine, me apron-clad and constantly baking apple pies on a picturesque AGA, like a sort of rustic Nigella!

And when I lived on my own there, and had no access to a car due to injury or illness, I had a clear insight into some of the worrying isolation that people live in, with no transport links to the shops, medical support, or friends for simple connection.

Striving for a sense of community

I am passionate about the idea that nobody living in the countryside – where they want to live, where they make their living, where their family has perhaps had a long history in the area, where they do important work to sustain the land and the wildlife and provide food for the country – should be alone. Emotional and physical wellbeing is maintained by community – by people feeling known, loved and supported; by people having a sense of purpose within that community; by people feeling safe; by people having places and set-ups in which to have fun and relax, even if that is comedians trying to start their career with a terrible sketch show! If community is the key to living well, then everyone needs to be connected and that means practical changes to many rural areas, from transport to technology.

But these challenges, however frustrating, and at times upsetting, actually shine a light on all the reasons we adore the countryside. That is, remoteness may mean difficulty with connectivity, but that remoteness has so much to

celebrate – the peace, the space, the nature – all of
which support holistic wellbeing (there are endless
studies on the positive effect of beauty on the nervous
system), as well as providing visitors from the city with a
much-needed refuge and, in some areas, healthy tourism.

Villages may be getting more cut off and village halls
and churches may have less attendance and need repair,
but they are still standing, and they have such beauty,
such rich history, individual purposes and character
– they are communities ready to be rebuilt. Everyone
living rurally, despite the difficulties, is there for unique,
beloved and vital reasons and therefore deserves respect,
understanding and support. Our countryside is one of
the most wonderful things about our little island and
I admire everyone who is a part of it. I really hope this
guide provides some tips to help necessary changes
happen so that life becomes more connected, freer,
fruitful (literally and metaphorically), peaceful and joyful.

With much love to all my fellow bumpkins!

Miranda Hart

IT'S ALL ABOUT
COMMUNITY

An increasing number of rural residents are flexing their community muscles to revitalise their villages. Their mantra? Don't look at what you're losing, make the most of what you've got! And that starts with passion and people...

In the spring of 2018, The Prince's Countryside Fund commissioned an online survey to inform its report, Recharging Rural, and tap into the experiences of rural communities across the UK. An impressive 3,098 responses came back, with people sharing their concerns and achievements, and highlighting how they're facing the challenges of remote living.

The good news? Communities are taking action themselves and of the 550 ongoing projects highlighted, many supported by The Prince's Countryside Fund, the most common are physical community hubs. That's somewhere for people to gather together – be it in halls, pubs, cafés, or at events, classes and workshops – and it's the people in these communities making it happen. Sometimes, though, the first hurdle to launching any project is being brave enough to put your head above the parapet and say: 'Hey, let's do something'.

Power to the people

The next challenge is getting people involved, capturing their attention and exploring your community's needs, resources and skills sets. Early barriers to gaining interest in a project can be as simple as a fear of meetings. Some people are just plain scared of saying the wrong thing – or they equate meetings with the business world – so remember to stress that listening is good, too. Not everyone has to be vocal.

Whatever you want to influence, your project needs to have a clear, shared vision. Locality, the national network supporting community organisations in England, suggests you initially ask yourselves these five questions...

THE NEXT STEP...
Locality has a helpful Getting Started section and tools at mycommunity.org.uk

1 **Who** is our community?
2 **What** are we trying to achieve?
3 **What** sort of organisation do we need?
4 **What** is our plan for our community project?
5 **How** much money will we need to develop our idea?

Driving enthusiasm

Great ideas can take time to come to fruition and the last thing you want is commitment fatigue before you've achieved anything, especially if you're depending on the same familiar, and willing, faces. People Power, a report from the Commission on the Future of Localism in 2017, revealed one of the core challenges of community projects is to ensure they are based on 'broad participation, involving not just the "loudest voices".' There is no fixed script that suits every community, but these ideas can help you get more people to sign up to an idea...

- **Organise talks/workshops** at every opportunity to explain your vision/plan
- **Use online media** Set up a Facebook group, post on local neighbourhood networks such as Nextdoor, or via environmental groups such as Freecycle, where you know people are already tuned in to the community
- **Send press releases** to local papers, and local radio and TV stations
- **Print and deliver leaflets** with information sheets, or distribute questionnaires
- **Engage the parish council** (if you have one)

CARING AND SHARING
The shop in New Galloway in south-west Scotland was saved from closure, and opened in refurbished premises in August 2018

£22.6 BILLION

The estimated annual value of volunteers helping UK charities

THE NEXT STEP...
For more information on the work of 10,000 village halls across England and their volunteers, go to acre.org.uk

Finding a place to meet

With the closure of rural post offices and shops, the village hall might be the only place for people to meet, yet many committees face challenges in managing their buildings, something ACRE (Action with Communities in Rural England), a network of 38 charitable local development agencies, knows all too well. The ACRE Network's village hall service supports the 80,000 volunteers that run rural halls and community buildings across England. The main challenges facing these groups are usually funding, getting enough volunteers on board and finding people willing to take on the responsibility of managing the building.

Members of ACRE Network share experiences on anything from community safety and energy-saving ideas, to the implications of legislation for rural communities. 'Our work can cover everything from advising a village hall how to change its governing document, to helping them find legal advice on their boundary issue,' says Deborah Clarke, who has provided the Village Hall Information & Advice Service to the network since 2000. ACRE also launched the annual Village Halls Week in January 2018 to build interest and encourage volunteers – because community ventures are so often all about the volunteers. 'You can have a building,' says Deborah, 'but without local people to run and manage it, then it's just an empty shell.'

Photography: Flick Humphrey, ACRE

IN OUR COMMUNITY
UPPER TEESDALE, COUNTY DURHAM

> Many customers pull up the chair from our community computer nearby and settle down for a chat while being served at the post office. Coming to see us has become part of their routine

The Upper Teesdale Agricultural Support Services (UTASS) in County Durham began in the 1990s to help reduce loneliness and stress among farmers, but has gradually grown to address challenges facing everyone living in a rural community. These are keenly felt in Teesdale, which is in the top 2% of the most deprived areas in England for access to services and housing.

Today, UTASS has more than 1,400 members from 416 farming families and its work includes running a community group, bulk-buying oil to save money for nearly 300 households and facilitating the postal service for the whole area. When the village post office closed in 2017, people living at the top of the Dales had to make a 45-mile trip to post a parcel, so the question was asked – could UTASS help? The answer was yes, and in April 2018 post office services began running one morning and one afternoon a week from the UTASS premises in Middleton-in-Teesdale.

Amanda Cooper, who lives on a remote Teesdale smallholding, is an outreach worker for the post office at UTASS. 'I only wish we could provide more hours, but on the two half-days we are there customers can pay bills and return items ordered online, while accessing support. We provide banking facilities for all the main banks and people can even leave things such as passports and vehicle tax for processing at the main branch and collect them later. Many regular customers, residents and local businesses rely on us now.'

IDENTIFY YOUR NEEDS

Your strongest asset is your village and the people in it – but where to start?

For the Wereham Village Hall committee, planning was key, so they...

- **Consulted with the community**, user groups and focus groups – everything from a reminiscent focus group for older people to a hands-on pasta class for adults not in work.
- **Did a door-to-door survey** to clarify which activities and services might resolve people's problems.
- **Created a Friends of... group** for people who enjoy volunteering, but didn't want the commitment of being a trustee.
- **Asked intended user groups to put representatives forward** to stand as trustees on the committee, believing everyone can have a voice and add value.

'**E**ngaging with your community is crucial to find out what people need,' says Victoria Gray, chair of the management committee that opened a new community hub through the Wereham Village Hall charity in Norfolk. 'The former WWI wooden building was beyond repair and structurally at risk, but we didn't want to lose the asset, so we embarked on a super-ambitious project to secure funding for a replacement.' Finance for the £1 million project came from a variety of sources, including the Big Lottery Fund and the Borough Council of King's Lynn & West Norfolk, and the new hall opened in 2018.

Since the new hall launch weekend, Victoria describes the local engagement as amazing. 'It has lifted our community and those of the villages around us. People are proud of the facility and excited by the opportunities it offers, including a partnership with Norfolk Community Learning Services to run community courses as part of their annual programme.'

Photography: John Millard

HOW TO DRAW UP A CONSULTATION FORM

To measure support, the Wereham Village Hall group devised a number of questions for a survey which was delivered to every household. Among other things, it asked residents whether they would be prepared to pay an increase via the Parish Precept (Council Tax) to help fund the charity. These are the sort of questions they included, which you could adapt and add to for your own village.

1 What do you like about living in [your village name]
- [ ] not being isolated
- [ ] having lots to do
- [ ] being independent
- [ ] well-kept village
- [ ] sense of wellbeing
- [ ] community spirit
- [ ] accessible to all

2 What do you dislike?
- [ ] feeling vulnerable
- [ ] feeling bored
- [ ] adults can't socialise
- [ ] children can't socialise
- [ ] no community spirit

3 What could [your village project] do to resolve these issues?
- [ ] toddler group
- [ ] youth club
- [ ] community hub
- [ ] regular post office
- [ ] adult education
- [ ] internet café
- [ ] social-care support groups
- [ ] indoor sports
- [ ] lunch club
- [ ] dances/events

4 Do you feel fit and healthy?

5 Would you attend keep fit/health promotion activities if they were offered in the village?

6 How do you view your access to community transport – good or poor?

7 Is there anything you travel out of [your village name] for that you would like to do in the village?

8 Do you have your own transport?

9 Where do you buy everyday groceries?

10 How do you get there?

11 What problems does this cause you?

12 Do you often run out of essential supplies?

13 Which post office do you use?

14 How do you get there?

15 What problems does this cause you?

16 Which age groups do you and the people in your home belong to? Under 16/16-25/26-45/46-65/65+

17 Would you like to join the Friends of [your village project] Volunteer Group?

18 Would you be interested in learning more about the new [your village project], supporting a focus group, or supporting the project at a later date?

GETTING PEOPLE TOGETHER
Sometimes a community just needs a little social glue to help bind it together.

3,900

The number of residents served by the Northern Fells Rural Development Group over an area of more than 200 square miles

In the upland region of north Cumbria, Village Agents are the eyes and ears of the community. Part of the Northern Fells Rural Development Group, which grew out of HRH The Prince of Wales's Rural Revival Projects and was launched in 2002, these agents organise activities and events, as well as visiting people at home.

After two months' training, Philippa Groves started seeing clients as a Village Agent in 2010. 'I've dealt with serious problems, from bereavement and alcohol addiction to Blue Badge applications and finding someone a mate for their duck!' she says. 'We signpost people to the help they may need and, if we can't help, we often know someone who can.' Support also includes assessments on energy supply, health and safety, and eligibility for benefits, and initiatives like the C.R.A.F.T. Club (Can't Remember A Flipping Thing), which helps with understanding memory loss. The Village Agents have set up numerous activities to combat social isolation in their region, which could be replicated in your village, including...

- **A surplus apple scheme** The first year it collected five tons of apples which would otherwise have gone to waste and the scheme sold the juice that was processed.
- **A men-in-sheds workshop**, held in an old water wheel room. It became so popular with a local dementia group, it found new premises and now employs a shed-master.
- **Singing just for fun**, which has morphed into a choir called 'Pitch up & Sing, Good in Parts' and now joins up with other local groups for performances.

Everybody needs good neighbours
Another good way to bring people back into the community is via the Good Neighbours Scheme, a nationwide initiative supported by ACRE. Seventeen of ACRE's members take part in the scheme, which is established and run by locals. It's like a social safety net,

Photography: Libby Graham

BUILDING
FRIENDSHIPS
The men-in-sheds
workshop from the
Northern Fells Rural
Development Group

putting volunteers in touch with people who need help,
from DIY and gardening tasks, to filling in forms
or just befriending.

Rebecca Breakwell advises on Good Neighbours
schemes for Northamptonshire ACRE. 'We have about
10 schemes and they all differ,' she says. 'Some mainly
offer social events and befriending. Others prefer to do
household tasks or pass on information such as warning
against doorstep scams. It depends on what comes back
from their community research. The co-ordinator
probably does the most work, taking and making calls,
and this can often be done by someone who would
otherwise be unable to work – so that they can play an
integral role – and it's a lovely way to combat loneliness.'

- **How are they set up?** A Good Neighbours Scheme is
often led by the parish council, but it doesn't have to
be and isn't going to add to the clerk's duties. It is
a separately constituted body.
- **What's the first step?** Form a steering group, five or
six people from the village hall committee, the parish
council or perhaps someone already running lunch
clubs. Distribute surveys to establish the community's
needs and the level of potential volunteers.
- **Do we need DBS checks?** You have to make a
judgement in each case, depending on the role. If
you're shopping for elderly people or taking them to
medical appointments, you may need a check. If you're
mending a fence or clearing snow, you may not.

THE NEXT STEP...
For tips on how to
recruit and manage
volunteers, plus
advice on drawing up
Volunteer Agreements,
check out the NCVO
(The National
Council for Voluntary
Organisations) at
knowhow.ncvo.org.uk

Making a Difference to Rural Communities Throughout Suffolk

Tel/Fax: 01379 855 338
enquiries@ruralcoffeecaravan.org.uk
www.ruralcoffeecaravan.org.uk

AV53 GKF

INSTANT SOCIAL SPACE
All the Rural Coffee Caravan needs is somewhere to park up and space for a table and a few chairs

Driving change

Not everyone wants, or needs, to log on to a laptop to feel connected to the outside world. For many people in isolated locations, the best information doesn't come through Google, but is delivered via a welcome cuppa, a slice of cake and an empathetic ear.

The Rural Coffee Caravan has been parking up in remote villages in rural Suffolk since 2003, offering the elderly, young parents and carers information, support and amazing homemade cakes. Help can include benefits or debt advice, how to access agencies and services, information on fuel poverty, or even how to apply for funding to set up their own coffee mornings.

The service is run by 50 volunteers, with one full-time and two part-time staff. Funding comes from a variety of sponsors, including one district council, plus it was one of 126 organisations to benefit from the government's Building Connections Fund in England.

'We've helped a similar scheme start in Kent, and are liaising with groups in Lincolnshire and Leicestershire,' says director Ann Osborn. 'We're happy to talk to anyone interested in starting a mobile coffee caravan because it's a very repeatable model. Once you have the van, the funding and the volunteers in place, it's a great way to create a social space in a rural place.'

Spreading the word

Community newsletters can be a lifeline, too. Over the Bridges (OTB) is the Church and Community Magazine for Upper Coquetdale, Northumberland, published 10 times a year, delivered to every household and also available online. It's published by a subsidiary committee of Upper Coquetdale Churches Together, which comprises 10 churches across four denominations that have all signed a formal covenant that states 'so as not to do separately what might be done together'.

Not just a hub of church news, its 40-plus pages cover everything from access to bereavement services and outreach postal services, to updates on the campaign against local hospital closures. 'The aim is to look forward positively and promote community engagement,' says editor Louise Kirkwood. 'One recent editorial initiative was to source more content relevant to young people and children. Three local schools and a nursery have agreed to send twice-yearly articles and/or pictures and youth groups are starting to submit short articles, too.

'A dedicated group of 70, mostly retired, volunteers bundles the copies in one of the churches and then distributes them door to door,' says Louise. 'One really positive side effect is that many of the volunteers develop a pastoral role themselves, through calling on neighbours they might not otherwise have met.'

Over the Bridges shared these facts for any community thinking of starting its own newsletter:

Getting the news out there
- OTB has a print run of 2,300 copies, delivered free to 2,120 homes, plus shops, churches, the GP's surgery and the art gallery.
- Digital downloads average 100 per month.

Paying its way
- Total annual running costs are around £27,000.
- The newsletter's main income comes from 90 commercial advertisers.

Print v digital
- Readers of the print version of OTB are often retired people who read it from cover to cover.
- Digital readers tend to be researchers, expats or younger readers looking for specific items.

THAT'S SUCH A COOL IDEA...

Does your area have a Community Fridge? It's a great way to save on food waste and get to know your neighbours better.

- **The very first Community Fridge was set up in Derbyshire in 2016 to redistribute good food to the community and cut down on waste.**
- **Today, there are more than 50 across the UK, with the aim of doubling that figure by 2020.**
- **In the first three months of the Community Fridge Network, over 21,000 kg of food was redistributed across 32 Community Fridges.**

Volunteer or set up your own Community Fridge at hubbub.org.uk

PUTTING THE
HEART
BACK INTO THE
VILLAGE

A village needs somewhere for
people to meet, to chat, to celebrate,
to share... Which is why rural
communities are rolling up their
sleeves, raising funds and saving,
or creating, social hubs for
everyone to enjoy

Historically, village life revolved around the village hall, the pub, the post office, the church, or the shop. But with so many closures, losing the simple things everyone took for granted – like meeting others while posting a letter, or catching up over a pint – has left many villagers disconnected. But it has also prompted others into action...

S even out of 10 villages in England no longer have a shop and, at the end of last year, the Office of National Statistics revealed the number of pubs in the UK had fallen from 52,500 in 2001 to 38,815. Both of these figures have a huge impact on rural communities, which already have limited places to shop and socialise. But who's to say you can't have a library in the back bar of the local, or a post office in a church?

Fortunately, plenty of people in rural or remote locations are gathering together with likeminded folk and seizing the initiative to prove that multi-use spaces are the future of rural living.

Launched in 2001, Pub is The Hub does what it says on the tin – it supports pub owners, breweries and licensees to put, or keep, the village pub at the heart of the community. It's a not-for-profit organisation and its work comes in many guises, from helping privately owned or community-owned pubs to offer a digital hub in an unused room, to taking ownership of a much-loved inn that's in danger of closing. The benefits of these projects are invaluable, from accessing essential services, to helping provide new skills for local residents.

In February this year, The Lamarsh Lion, Essex, opened its new café and community games room converted from an adjacent barn, with the help of a grant from the Pub is The Hub Community Services Fund. The same fund helped The Green Dragon at Market Lavington, Wiltshire, launch a digital hub in the skittle alley at the rear of the pub, to help encourage older residents to get online and develop their digital skills.

£337,650

The average cost of setting up a community pub

THE NEXT STEP...
For ideas on ways to save your pub or turn it into a multi-use venue, go to pubisthehub.org.uk

IN OUR COMMUNITY
ELSDON, NORTHUMBERLAND

> We're offering shifts to students in the holidays, and to people on zero-hours contracts elsewhere to help boost their incomes. We're not community owned, but the pub is the hub of our community

Living across the green from 18th-century village pub Bird in Bush in Elsdon, Northumberland, Katie Bland and Stephen Shaw witnessed its slow decline and eventual closure in 2015. 'That's when the heart of the village died,' says Katie. 'We have no shop and no post office, which meant people were hardly going out or meeting up. That was when we decided to buy the pub.'

The couple initially received a Community Services Fund grant for a mini library and digital hub from Pub is The Hub, which directed them to The Prince's Countryside Fund for a grant to build a restaurant kitchen and bunkhouse. 'With a fabulous chef in our new kitchen, we've become a destination pub,' says Katie. 'We're not on the main road, so people are making a point to visit us, plus we've branched out from just doing live music to hosting events and weddings, too.'

The pub has also launched a library in a purpose-built alcove in the bar with an internet-enabled laptop and shelves for books.

'People don't just come for a drink, but for a coffee and a catch-up, so it helps alleviate rural isolation,' says Katie. 'I like to think we're the human interface of the village.'

What we learned...

1 Be sure to meet all the procedures, policies and standards for your building, such as building regulations or cellar management.

2 Share your plans with the relevant bodies, from the fire service to environmental health. Don't wait for them to come to you.

3 Rather than build a costly website, use social media and your rural resources. Word of mouth is very powerful!

Photography: Pub Is The Hub

85

The number of community pubs trading across the UK with more than 15,500 shareholders*

WHAT IS AN ASSET OF COMMUNITY VALUE (ACV)?

You can nominate buildings or other assets as an ACV if its current use (or recent past use) benefits the social wellbeing of your local community. Once listed with your local authority, you will be informed if it is listed for sale within the five-year listing period under the Community Right to Bid. Discover more at mycommunity.org.uk

TAKING CONTROL OF THE FUTURE

In some areas, the way forward is community ownership.

In 2012, a group of villagers from Bamford in the Peak District organised a village meeting and set up Bamford Community Society (BCS) to stop what they felt was a village in decline. They had already lost their GP surgery and now the last pub in the village was up for sale. Having registered The Anglers Rest as an Asset of Community Value – one of the first pubs in the country to be registered under the newly enacted Localism Act – they started working on a business plan to buy it.

The group sought support from the Plunkett Foundation, a UK-wide charity committed to helping communities create sustainable initiatives and thriving businesses. This enabled them to set up a share offer to buy the pub, as well as producing a business plan to ensure its long-term viability.

'It seemed improbable, but we had to give it a go,' says BCS society secretary Sally Soady. 'There were relatively few community pubs around at the time, but the ones we spoke to were really helpful and supportive and we all had a can-do attitude. So we produced and promoted a share offer and eventually raised £263,000 in community shares, with 80% of our shareholders living within a five-mile radius.'

A new village focal point

With a further commercial loan of £90,000, the society took over The Anglers Rest in October 2013.

'Nearly six years on and the pub, the Rest Café and the post office are still open,' says Sally. 'Although things are challenging financially, the village now has a focal point, with regular exhibitions, live music, art exhibitions and food events. Around 75% of our expenditure goes into the local economy, including 20-25 staff, which is fantastic as many of these are young people working part-time in their first paid job.'

*Community Pubs: A Better Form of Business 2018/Plunkett Foundation

The Bamford Community Society made the impossible possible by...

- **Spreading the word** with open meetings, drop-in sessions, leaflets (every home received around a dozen!), website, Facebook and Twitter updates, and interviews with local press, TV and radio.
- **Engaging the community** The society asked what people wanted and it became clear that a café would be popular, so this was added to the business plan.
- **Harnessing the skills** on the steering group and within the community – finance, legal, building, marketing – and maximising the input of people with strong connections to the community.
- **Encouraging the wider community** to get involved by volunteering to help with ad hoc jobs such as painting, gardening, joinery, accountancy tasks, or booking bands and artists.
- **Seeking advice** from existing community-run pub groups and organisations including the Plunkett Foundation, Pub is The Hub and Co-operatives UK.

OPEN TO ALL
The Anglers Rest won the Heart of the Community Award at the 2018 Accessible Derbyshire Awards

80%

of the members of Bamford Community Society say they have got to know new people since taking ownership of The Anglers Rest

NEW DELIVERIES
Postman Pat would scarcely recognise the settings for many of today's rural post offices.

31%

of rural residents use a post office at least once a week*

One of the key pillars of any community is the post office, especially in areas where bank services have been withdrawn. The Government Access Criteria requires Post Office Ltd to make sure 95% of the population is within three miles of a post office and, according to a Citizens Advice Report from 2017, more than 98% are. But even three miles is a distance if you don't have a car and buses are rare or non-existent. And that criteria doesn't mean the service has to be open every day.

The changing face of rural post offices means that some are now run from other businesses, such as shops, or are hosted via pubs or churches, often with a limited range of services. Blaenavon in South Wales has a post office in its arts, crafts and haberdashery shop, and Allonby in Cumbria even had one in a fish and chip shop! In other instances, a sub-postmaster travels to some kind of community hall, hub or centre – complete with the necessary technology ready to plug in – to offer a limited number of hours a week.

HELP, our post office is under threat!

Thanks to St Mary Church (aka Stow Minster) in Stow, Lincolnshire, the village now has a pop-up post office in the North Transept, otherwise known as the Becket Chapel. The service is provided by the owner of a full-time post office at North Wheatley, Nottinghamshire, who has responsibility for other pop-up post offices in the area. Churchwarden David Justham led the group that made the pop-up happen. 'It has proved to be very popular, attracting customers not only from Stow, but also from nearby villages,' he says. 'And as a result of our positive experience, we've been able to advise a number of other churches within the diocese about the process of developing a hosted post office of their own.'

Thanks to funding from the players of People's Postcode Lottery, The Prince's Countryside Fund has given 34 grants to help tackle isolation in rural areas, ranging from a community brewery in Essex to a film and arts festival in Northumberland

*Rural Post Office Use://citizensadvice.org.uk

HOW STOW MINSTER MADE IT HAPPEN...

JAN 2014
Stow's full-time post office was closed

MAY 2014
The civil Stow Parish Council got a letter from the national Post Office asking if there was a venue in the village for a 'hosted' post office. As the church was the only public building, the parish council asked the Parochial Church Council of Stow if the church could reply.

JUNE 2014
The rector, churchwardens and the PCC treasurer met with representatives from the Post Office and the civil Stow Parish Council to explore the possibilities of the church hosting a pop-up.

MAR 2015
The pop-up post office opened in the North Transept of Stow Minster, operating three half-days per week.

2014/15
During this time there was...
• A public consultation about the prospect of a pop-up post office.
• The development of a bishop's licence to allow the terms under which the post office could operate within the church.
• An application to Royal Mail to have Stow Minster registered as a postal address.
• An application, via a faculty – the church's equivalent of obtaining planning permission – to allow for the installation of a telephone line, a dedicated power supply and to confirm the bishop's licence.
• Agreement to the terms and conditions required by the national Post Office.

MORE THAN JUST A SHOP

When a much-needed shop is about to close, the first thought is... What can *we* do?

346

community shops in the UK are owned by 61,000 shareholders*

Many villages simply want to preserve the status quo – buy the shop as a community and carry on as usual – but, as these two villages discovered, community ownership can bring far more benefits than just milk and papers.

Taking control in Cornwall

When the closure of the commercial shop was announced in the village of St Tudy, north Cornwall, in February 2011, a group immediately formed to find ways to react. With no public transport, the impact would mean a loss of independence for many locals, particularly older people. The group approached The Prince's Countryside Fund for a grant and things moved quickly – from closing its doors on 21 April 2011, it reopened as a community project just a day later! It has also brought together many people volunteering in the shop who wouldn't usually socialise. And it has given volunteer Sue Dibble another new focus – as the village's champion jam-maker.

'I used to make jam for the church fete, but many people who grow soft fruit started to bring me extra, as there is always such an excess,' she says. 'At first, I made

WINNING FORMULAS
Right: St Tudy was first in the Rural Community Ownership Awards 2016, South West Region. Opposite page: Something for every generation at Hallbankgate Hub

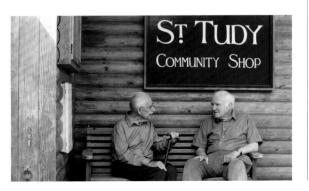

*Plunkett Foundation

half a dozen jars for the shop, which we displayed in a little basket but, like Topsy, it grew. Now the shop often has something in the region of 250 jars on its shelves!'

Keeping the legacy going

There's been a co-operative shop in Hallbankgate, Cumbria, for 130 years, but when the last one closed in 2015 the locals set up a community benefit society to take over the running of it. Raising money through share issues and funding, including from The Prince's Countryside Fund, they reopened in 2016. Shareholders now receive a social dividend of their investment through a popular community-run shop and café, with a crucial library link and weekly postal link. Turnover is growing and the hub is a lifesaver for people without transport. While the society's next big step is to recruit a full-time manager, volunteers are still their lifeblood.

'We have wised up to the fact that we don't just need people to serve behind the counter or make food,' says committee secretary Sheila Pinder. 'We need volunteers for specific roles, ie, someone to be a library link co-ordinator, or to take care of the fire-extinguisher safety testing. Not all roles involve spending time with customers, which not everyone wants to do. Working behind the scenes is really valuable, too.'

TURNING
SURVIVE
INTO THRIVE
Hallbankgate Hub committee shares its top tips for success...

1 At the early stages of planning, when you're trying to reach consensus, find an impartial chairperson with some business experience but no direct involvement in the area.

2 Be careful not to underestimate the time things take. It's easy to miscalculate how much energy a project needs, which can exhaust your volunteers and make them cautious of how much they will commit to in future.

3 Think about your knowledge management. As old committee members leave and new ones join, knowing who did and donated what – not just funding but in terms of goodwill – is very important.

IN OUR COMMUNITY
ENNERDALE, CUMBRIA

‘ We originally thought we'd use the old workshop as a shop, with quaint crates of local veg and fruit outside, until our funders said "Why don't you knock it down and build something new?" So we did! ’

Believing in innovation rather than restoration, one community in Cumbria built its own community spirit, quite literally. The villagers of Ennerdale were first prompted to set up a co-operative to buy the last pub in the village which was in decline.

Motivated by their success, the co-operative embarked on new plans for a shop, community room and café, none of which the village had.

'The Forestry Commission gave us an old workshop site at a peppercorn rent of £1 a year, and we raised £730,000 through funders including the Big Lottery Fund,' says Peter Maher, who led the project.

Over a five-year period, the old workshop site was demolished, the builders moved in and The Gather opened in 2016. Three-quarters of the staff across the shop, café and community

room are volunteers, including the group which makes all the cakes sold in the café. It also employs 10 part-time staff.

'It did well from the start,' says Peter. 'We're making a profit and we continue to enjoy the support of the community – our retired doctor in his mid-80s turns up every week to do his stint at washing up! People now come from far and wide. It's not just for locals – The Gather is a destination.'

What we learned...

1 You need positive leadership, or you can end up in circular discussions.

2 A project must reflect what the community wants, so continue consulting throughout.

3 Don't underestimate the task of raising funding. The process can be long and complex.

HELPING PEOPLE HELP THEMSELVES

In areas where people are spread over a wide area, one shop or hall is not always enough.

This is something that Community Action Northumberland (CAN) knows only too well. Northumberland is one of the most sparsely populated counties in England – with just 63 people per square kilometre – which is why community development officer Christine Nicholls initiated the Warm Hubs project three years ago, with funding from Northern Gas Networks. The project works with 26 community buildings across the region to offer people a friendly environment to enjoy a cup of tea, a hot lunch, or a social activity. Each hub is run for local people by local people, with CAN offering advice and support to make sure that each building:

• is fit for purpose, this includes risk assessments, energy audits and accessibility checks
• has the right licences and insurance in place
• recruits volunteers who receive ongoing training

Because CAN is working with volunteers in their own buildings – from churches to community halls – the initial outlay is minimal. Any building can join the scheme for free and the funding pays for things like energy audits, dementia assessments, plus training in everything from first aid to food safety. CAN also helps groups apply for funding for refurbishment from other sources and that has brought in over £500,000 in additional grants for the buildings over the past three years. At the other end of the scale, CAN makes small grants available for more immediate needs, such as a set of crockery.

Other ACRE Network members are picking up on the idea – Christine ran a pilot in Hampshire – and it is possible the Warm Hubs model will eventually be rolled out nationally. 'We're not precious about our scheme,' says Christine. 'The more Warm Hubs, the merrier!'

40%

of Northumberland's population lives in small towns, villages, hamlets and isolated dwellings

SCHOOL'S OUT, BUT WE'RE NOT!

Despite a three-year 'save our school' campaign which reached judicial review at the High Court, Hermon Village School, Pembrokeshire, was closed in 2006.

MAKING THINGS HAPPEN

'There was a lot of anger over the closure of the school and an equal amount of passion for the new project. Those two emotions are a good combination!'
Cris Tomos, Canolfan Hermon

Determined to keep this building as the hub of the community, locals formed a committee and set up a community benefit society (formerly known as an industrial and provident society), launching a share offer to raise funds to buy the site from the council. This netted them £49,000, which they combined with funds from the Welsh Government's Community Facility Activities Programme to buy the old school.

Cris Tomos, whose children went to the school, was on the committee that made it happen. He was working at the County Voluntary Council at the time and knew there were many successful community projects out there and theirs could be one of them. 'We approached The Hive, a support programme delivered by Co-operatives UK, and they held our hands through the process,' he says. 'They have a great website and gave us all the templates we needed for our constitution and share issue.'

It soon became obvious that the school site wasn't big enough for all the groups and activities that wanted it, so they secured additional funding from the Big Lottery Fund. The development of the new timber-framed extension for Canolfan Hermon (Hermon Centre) began in 2011 and it opened in 2013. Cris Tomos has this advice:

- **Make study visits to similar projects** to learn from their experiences and avoid pitfalls.
- **Produce a realistic business plan** A community benefit society is a business and has to pay its way.
- **Show potential shareholders they are investing** in a long-term asset, not just a concept.

THE NEXT STEP...
Find out more about setting up a co-operative at uk.coop/the-hive

10 THINGS TO INCLUDE IN A BUSINESS PLAN

Taking over any enterprise as a community needs a business plan, both to hone your own understanding of the project and to prove to funders that you have a viable concept. Your steering group or parish council may have members with relevant business expertise, but the Plunkett Foundation, which supports rural community business initiatives, has a range of guides to help, including a business plan template. When drawing up a business plan, consider covering these areas…

1 Your mission, aims and objectives
What is the need you are hoping to meet?

2 Your organisation
Who is running it? What is the background to the group? What does membership entail?

3 Your products, services and activities
What are you going to do/produce/sell? How does it benefit the local community?

4 Your market and your strategy
Who is the target customer and what evidence do you have that you can succeed in this market?

5 Your competitors
Who are they and what are their strengths and weaknesses in comparison to your model?

6 The resources you need
How many people and what facilities will you need? How much will it cost? Where will the finance come from?

7 Your revenue
How much of your product or service do you intend to sell? What is your estimated income? Will you make a profit?

8 Your targets, outputs and outcomes
What will success look like? How will you measure the results (for example, the number of people who will benefit)?

9 The risks you face
What are they and how will you control or mitigate these? What are the liabilities of investors and members?

10 Your budget
Financial forecasts.

THE NEXT STEP…
Find an introduction to Preparing a Business Plan and more at plunkett.co.uk/information

BECAUSE THERE'S NO PLACE LIKE HOME

The key to meeting rural housing needs is for villages across the UK to work with housing associations and local authorities to create local homes for local people

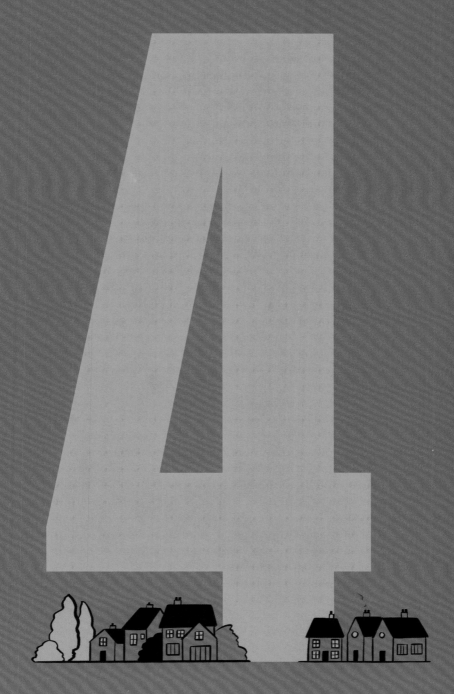

The countryside may often appear to offer a peaceful, rustic charm, but for all its picture-postcard appeal to the outside world, it's an increasingly challenging place to find affordable housing.

'In looking to the future of the countryside, housing is, of course, a key requirement. There is a particular problem of finding ways for elderly farmers and farm workers to retire with dignity, in their own community, just as there is to house the new entrants who will provide the future of farming.'
HRH The Prince of Wales, writing as guest editor of Country Life to celebrate his 70th birthday, November 2018

8%

In villages with a population of 3,000 or fewer, the supply of social housing is 8%, compared with 19% for urban areas*

Many factors feed into this housing shortage, not least the gap between rural house prices and rural wages. In April 2018, the Office of National Statistics revealed the average house-price-to-income ratio across England and Wales had risen to 7.77 to 1. This effectively means buyers have to find nearly eight times their annual salary to buy an average house. In the rural central Lake District area, however, that house-price-to-income ratio jumps to 12.1 to 1.

Housing associations play a huge role in building and managing affordable housing, but when they are trying to cover vast areas of rural landscape, or island communities, they can't always be expected to know or understand the needs of every village. They may focus more on what might be possible when land becomes available, rather than what's needed where. Which is where community-led projects and Community Land Trusts (CLTs) come in, by identifying needs and driving awareness.

Communities taking the lead

One successful collaboration completed in late 2018 was a development of 12 affordable homes (a mix of one, two and three-bedroom houses and bungalows) in the Somerset village of Mark. A group of residents set up the Mark Community Land Trust in 2015, to assess the area's needs and identify a site. They took their idea to South Western Housing Society (SWHS), a small social landlord with charitable status and, with funding from the Government's Homes England fund and Sedgemoor District Council, construction was completed in September 2018.

The Mark site consisted of homes for rent to applicants that could prove a close connection to the village. But not all of SWHS's developments are rent-only properties.

'At Cullompton, Devon, for instance, one of our biggest developments with 24 properties, a third were 50/50 shared ownership, so we got half of that money back,' says operations director Martin Carney. 'We've just taken ownership of land at Denbury, Devon, where we are building 10 properties – one will be a self-build, two will be shared ownership and seven will be for rented housing. Another scheme at Brent Knoll, Somerset, will have 15 properties and, of those, seven will be affordable rented properties, two will be shared ownership and six are going to be outright sales to help finance the scheme. Not every social housing provider does cross subsidy and outright sales, but it provides valuable funding towards the affordable housing, so it's a good model.'

SWHS also works closely with the local and parish councils on the criteria for housing allocation. 'Usually, the first criteria is that people have to have lived in the parish – and that's the parish, not the village,' says Martin. 'Sometimes a parish boundary can include two villages. Then it might be people who work in the parish, have close relatives there, or maybe used to live there but had to move because there wasn't anywhere affordable to live. As owners of social housing, we have a huge responsibility to work closely with the parish when putting allocation criteria together to ensure the village voice is heard.'

SMILES ALL ROUND
The launch of 12 new homes in the village of Mark, Somerset, in 2018

'Our community grants programme offers organisations with great housing solutions the chance to apply for grants of up to £50,000. So far we've given £4 million to more than 100 local projects across the UK, including some in rural locations.'
Rachel Smith, Nationwide Building Society

HOME HELP

'When it comes
to rural housing,
it takes a relatively
small number of
homes to help
cement that
community's
sustainability.
What you do
need is a range
of homes to meet
different needs.'
*Peter Moore,
Cornwall Rural
Housing Association*

THE NEXT STEP
Rural Housing Alliance
has a practical guide
for parish councils
looking into affordable
housing projects at
rsnonline.org.uk

Meeting local needs in Cornwall

Any community embarking on a housing project needs to know the wheels can turn slowly. When Cornwall Rural Housing Association (CRHA) sat down to talk to the communities across three islands in the Isles of Scilly in 2001, it was the start of a 10-year project. Each island has a population of 60-90 residents and there were concerns that one, at least, might become unviable because of its age profile and lack of affordable homes for families.

'The islanders approached us initially, so we met with the Duchy of Cornwall and the Council of the Isles of Scilly to jointly agree a strategy,' says chief executive Peter Moore. 'The challenge was how to convince the funding authorities that these developments were worth doing. That's more than half the battle. We basically got the scheme ready to go, so that we could take advantage of any funding if it should become available, and it did.'

The homes were the first social-housing properties on what are called the off-islands (Bryher, St Agnes and St Martin's) and the development in total consisted of six three-bedroom houses and one two-bedroom bungalow. Although they were expensive to build because of shipping and transport costs, the value to the community is obvious. 'The people in our properties make an important contribution to their communities,' says Peter. 'On the off-islands, one tenant owns the bakery, another has a restaurant and others run the post office and help with the boat services.' Over the last six years, 11 babies have also been born to families in the CRHA houses which, in turn, helps to keep local primary schools open.

'When it comes to rural housing, it takes a relatively small number of homes to help cement that community's sustainability,' says Peter. 'What you do need is a range of homes to meet different needs. Our last development featured eight homes with five different house types: two, three and four-bedroom houses, a bungalow for someone who needed level-access accommodation and a unit we call 1.5 bedrooms. Basically, it's a home for single people or childless couples, with a double bedroom and a small study room that can be used for working from home or other uses. It's important to remember that the needs of single people or couples without children are often overlooked or not met in villages.'

IN OUR COMMUNITY
ULVA FERRY, ISLE OF MULL

> ' There are high infrastructure costs when you're building on islands. Our quantity surveyor estimated building the same houses in central Scotland would have cost around 25% less '

In 2011, Ulva Ferry on the Isle of Mull was in danger of losing its school, which was down to four pupils. A lack of affordable housing meant the long-term population was in decline. A housing project started by Ulva School Community Association (USCA) and supported by Mull & Iona Community Trust (MICT) led to the building of two houses next to the school. They opened in 2017 and are occupied by two families, including six children, to help secure the future of the school.

'Finding funding and explaining why it costs so much is a challenge,' says MICT's housing project officer Helen MacDonald. 'To install private water supplies, you have to drill a borehole. Our first failed because it hit salt water. We'd drilled 70 metres then had to stop, but we still had to pay for it!'

Transportation is another issue. 'We have Road Equivalent Tariffs between the islands, which don't apply to commercial vehicles. If you come to Mull on the ferry in an 8-metre camper van, it costs £50 return. An 8-metre lorry carrying materials is £250.'

In 2014, MICT secured funding from the Scottish Land Fund to buy the land and bring in a project manager, which was Helen. 'We got £47,000 via fundraising, including one large donation,' says Helen. 'Argyll and Bute Council also agreed to a grant of £180,000. Most funders want you to have some funding in place before they release theirs, so we had to find that cash before we could get the contractor in. That's not unique to us – it's just another challenge.'

Photography: Johnny Barrington

For any community-led project, Rural Housing Scotland suggests keeping these stakeholders in the loop...

1 Local councillors These are the natural link to the services you need to engage, such as housing, planning and transport.

2 Local residents Including 'hard to reach' groups such as young people, who may not have thought about future housing needs.

3 Landowners They may be keen to provide land for a community project.

4 People who may like to return to the area Try reaching them by word of mouth, posters, social media and local press.

5 Schools and businesses Essential services will only remain if a community is able to maintain ratios of families with children or of working age.

The village of Sharnbrook, Bedfordshire, celebrated 13 new homes from Hastoe Housing Association in 2018 (above), consisting of five shared ownership, four outright sales and four affordable rented properties. A drop-in consultation was held prior to the planning application to take on board comments from local people, and the houses were built to the ultra-energy-efficient Passivhaus standard. This can lower fuel bills to as little as £150 a year.

'The Passivhaus standard is so important in a rural setting, where fuel poverty is often much higher than in urban communities,' says Hastoe regional development manager Isobel Wright. 'It significantly reduces fuel poverty at a stroke and builds affordability into the fabric of the building. It's a design feature that's particularly important for shared ownership and affordable rent homes, leaving residents with more money to cover other bills.'

Put your housing needs on the map

- **Be clear of your community's specific needs** and ask for external input to help gather evidence, such as a rural housing enabler (who can act between landowners, local authorities and housing associations). If there's little social housing in your area, people are unlikely to put their names on the housing register, which could suggest little need for development – when the opposite is true!

- **Gain the support of local businesses** to back your case for new developments by stressing how difficult it is to fill skilled positions. If candidates can't find local accommodation, that impacts on local economic growth.

- **Whip up support** from as many people as you can, from residents and the parish council to housing associations.

WHAT DOES IT MEAN?

Know your way around the jargon of housing development

AFFORDABLE HOUSING

Defined by the Rural Housing Alliance as homes for people on modest incomes who can't afford to buy or rent on the open market. This can include rental, ownership and part-ownership.

COMMUNITY LAND TRUST

A group set up by the community itself to develop and manage homes. CLTs ensure housing remains affordable, based on local earnings, not just for now, but for every future occupier.

COMMUNITY SELF-BUILD

Where a group of individuals and families come together to plan, design and build their own homes. Discover more, including site visits to ongoing projects, at communityselfbuild agency.org.uk

EXCEPTIONS SITES

Small sites used for affordable housing in perpetuity not otherwise available for housing. Could include local farmers and landowners, conservation areas, National Parks, greenfield sites and the Green Belt, as well as land owned by estates such as National Trust, the Church of England and The Crown Estate.

GREENFIELD SITE

Usually farmland not previously developed (not to be confused with Green Belt).

REASONABLE PREFERENCE ALLOCATION

A provision in the Localism Act 2011 regarding the allocation of schemes to give preference, for instance, to young families if the school is under threat, or local business employees.

BEYOND THE REACH OF LOCAL RESIDENTS

From holiday lets and Airbnb to the rise of second homes, properties not available to local people can squeeze out the young and push up prices.

3%

The stamp duty increase since 2016 for anyone buying a second home

A nother challenge to affordable rural housing is the rise in second homes – between 2000 and 2014, the number of adults who owned more than one home increased by 30%*. Of these, researchers found fewer than 4% of owners were letting out the properties, which suggests a lot of houses, flats and cottages are left empty for most or part of the year.

Effective neighbourhood planning

One county that has experienced this phenomenon more than others is Cornwall, famed for its beautiful landscapes and quaint seaside villages. And its dogged determination, it seems, ever since 83% of voters in a 2016 referendum in St Ives voted to adopt a Neighbourhood Plan that included a ban on any new properties being used as second homes. The decision was backed by a High Court ruling. The plan did only specify the ban on 'new homes' however, and figures compiled by estate agency Hamptons International show that nearly one in 10 of all houses bought in Cornwall in 2017 was for a second home.

But the idea of communities voting for Neighbourhood Plans to ban new builds being snapped up as second homes is catching on. In 2018, almost 90% of voters supported the Mevagissey Neighbourhood Plan to restrict new builds to permanent occupiers only. At the time, Cornwall Councillor for Mevagissey James Mustoe stressed that it 'wasn't about penalising second-home owners, who contribute a great deal to our economy, but about restoring the balance for local people'.

Because there's no place like home

Communities having their say

Not every development is community-led, and there are other ways you, as local residents, can have some input into commercial building projects in your area.

A Neighbourhood Plan, sometimes called a Neighbourhood Development Plan, is created by the parish council, town council, or a neighbourhood forum. It is different from a Local Plan, which is prepared by the local authority. A Neighbourhood Plan can be used to...

• help develop a shared vision for your neighbourhood
• help determine the size and type of housing development in your area
• detail priorities, such as the provision of low-cost housing or the preservation of green space
• choose where new homes, shops, offices and other developments should be built

A Community or Village Design Statement (VDS) is more concerned with the visual character of a village or neighbourhood. It's not about preventing development, so much as managing it effectively. Anyone in the village can take the lead in starting one up, and the main point is to get your VDS adopted as a supplementary planning document in the local plan for your area.

HOMES FOR
FARMING
FAMILIES
In 'Retirement Housing for Farmers in the UK', The Prince's Countryside Fund and its partners looked at housing problems in the sector. Suggested solutions include encouraging imaginative practices and proactive behaviour, as well as having negotiations with everyone from local planning authorities to farming families considering their future, as well as having discussions about landlord/ tenant relationships.
Jeremy Moody, The Central Association of Agricultural Valuers (CAAV)

THE NEXT STEP
Discover more about Neighbourhood Plans and Village Design Statements at planninghelp. cpre.org.uk

GETTING FROM
A-B

With cutbacks in services leading
to increased isolation, enterprising
community groups are putting their
foot firmly on the pedal to meet the
challenges of rural transport

When The Prince's Countryside Fund asked more than 3,000 respondents to define 'What is "remote" rural?', there are no prizes for guessing which answer came top – 'need a car to access anything'*. Yet an estimated 25% of people don't have access to a vehicle or don't drive, particularly among older people, leaving many communities high and dry...

Not surprisingly, with traditional rural bus services reduced or axed due to lack of funding, many people in villages have been increasingly isolated, with restricted access to other villages, towns and, most importantly, services. Fortunately, there are enterprising people from rural communities across the country who have found other ways to keep the wheels turning locally. Some are simple but practical ideas for individuals, such as the Wheels2Work schemes popping up across the country. The one delivered by the Shropshire Rural Communities Charity helps people get to work, training or job interviews by hiring out scooters and electric bikes for a three-month period, and at an affordable rate.

Others focus on running community transport solutions that rely on a mix of paid staff and volunteers.

6%

Rural bus mileage fell 6% between 2011/12 and 2016/17**

ALL ABOARD
The Little White Bus linking communities in North Yorkshire

'Recharging Rural.' "The future of rural bus services in the UK/bettertransport.org.uk. †Campaign for National Parks

One such example is The Little White Bus Community Minibus Service based in Hawes, North Yorkshire.

'Hawes is 17 miles from nowhere, 27 miles from somewhere and 35 miles from anywhere you can get something done,' says founder John Blackie, underlining the vital need for a bus connection in their community. 'When the service from Hawes to Scarsdale Station was withdrawn in 2011, we persuaded the county council to come out with a tender offer. We put in for a service based on using volunteers and one or two part-time drivers, they made a 16-seater minibus available to us, and we were off. I was the first volunteer driver.'

The Little White Bus now carries around 60,000 passengers a year on several routes in the deeply rural Upper Dales. It has 70 volunteers, eight paid part-time drivers and it runs 10 minibuses and a Land Rover 4x4 passenger carrier for specialist home-to-school journeys.

Alongside his work with the minibus service, John is a county, district and parish councillor – he has been described locally as 'indefatigable' – but believes you don't need his experience to make things happen. 'Once you have a small committee together, you can approach councillors at your county council,' he says. 'It's their job to keep your community viable and sustainable, and we've been lucky to have strong, continued support from ours.

'You do need a leader, no question, and you need a team that includes people you pay and people who do it for the love of it. Plus you need the ownership of the local community. I knew we had that when a fifth-generation farmer came up to me and said "That's good, our little white bus". It was the word *our* that said it all.

'It's important to identify the characteristics of your community. Up here it's self-reliance and independence with a cussed streak. We won't take no for an answer when there is even the remotest chance of a yes!'

Ticket to success

An alternative to volunteer-based community transport is to take over the running of services via a Community Interest Company (CIC), the way some groups have in the Yorkshire Dales. Friends of DalesBus is a voluntary organisation that manages a Bus Operating Fund to which passengers can make donations. These funds are then

ASK FOR HELP

'Once you have a small committee, you can approach councillors at your county council. It's their job to keep your community viable and sustainable, and we've been lucky to have strong, continued support from ours.'
John Blackie, The Little White Bus

£2 TO £2.50

The amount generated by buses in benefits to local communities for every £1 of local authority spend†

**WHAT IS A
COMMUNITY
INTEREST
COMPANY (CIC)?**
A CIC is a special type
of limited company,
designed for social
enterprises, that
benefits a community
rather than private
shareholders. It's more
lightly regulated than
a charity, but doesn't
have the benefits
of charitable status.
To set up a CIC,
you'll need:
• A 'community
  interest statement',
  explaining what
  your business
  plans to do.
• An 'asset lock'. This
  is a legal promise
  stating that the
  company's assets
  will only be used for
  its social objectives,
  and setting limits on
  the money it can pay
  to shareholders.
• A constitution.
• Approval from the
  CIC Regulator. Your
  application will
  automatically be
  sent to them.

THE NEXT STEP...
Learn how to register
a CIC at gov.uk

transferred, along with other fundraising, to the Dales & Bowland CIC, which operates various bus services in the Yorkshire Dales using two main professional operators, Arriva and Transdev. Sounds a bit complicated? Maybe, but it's a model that works and has been replicated in other areas. Colin Speakman is the founder of both Friends of DalesBus and D&BCIC.

'The CIC is a social enterprise with a board of eight unpaid volunteers, which acts exactly like a local authority or national park authority would, by designing services, specifying buses and setting timetables,' he explains. 'Friends of DalesBus, on the other hand, is more of our campaigning arm, fundraising through concerts and events, helping with marketing, even lobbying MPs on transport issues.'

Friends of DalesBus receives funding from sources such as West Yorkshire Combined Authority, National Parks and the National Trust. It has been going for over 20 years, growing the network from a single bus route from Ilkley to Skipton, to many routes today including the Harrogate/Nidderdale area and the Western Dales.

A similar, smaller organisation is Friends of Moorsbus in the North York Moors, another not-for-profit members organisation that runs a Bus Operating Fund with funds going to Moorsbus CIC. Since 2014, Moorsbus has covered 25-50% of its costs through fares and pass reimbursement, with the rest fundraised via council, Lottery grants and The Prince's Countryside Fund.

Colin Speakman believes all these rural services not only benefit local inhabitants and visitors to the National Park in a practical way, they help boost the local economy, too. 'Bus users spend more money because they can't just jump in the car and drive home,' he says. 'If they're waiting for the 5pm bus and it's raining, they're likely to be in the shop, the café, or the pub. They're good spenders!'

Transport on demand
Another innovation born from the lack of services has been the growth in demand-responsive transport (DRT), where routes are based around demand rather than a fixed timetable. In Lincolnshire, North Lincolnshire, Rutland, Peterborough and East Northants, CallConnect buses

IN OUR COMMUNITY
PLUCKLEY, KENT

' When you start out, yes, you do need someone with business skills on the team. It's important, but not too difficult. Anyone who can run a local shop would be more than capable of handling it! '

After continuous complaints about poor transport links between villages around Pluckley in Kent, Kent County Council (KCC) suggested villagers might want to set up something for themselves – so they did.

Co-founders Alan Davies and Tim Lee put together a business plan, lobbied for funding from KCC and Ashford Borough Council, and their community project, Wealden Wheels, was born. Two-thirds of their journeys now connect schools, older people, or the disabled around the villages of Pluckley, Charing, Chilham, Egerton and Smarden. The project is run as a car club, so each family, individual or group pays an annual membership (£10 for founding member villages, £15 for general membership).

Drivers must be DBS checked to drive the larger buses, although finding volunteers is an ongoing issue. 'A few do a lot and a lot do a little, but it all helps,' says Alan. 'Equally, we wouldn't be where we are today without our paid administrator – it's vital to have someone to look after the paperwork.'

Celebrity endorsement from local resident Vic Reeves (above) and his wife, Nancy, is also welcome, helping gain vital local press coverage.

A quarter of their business is now self-drive, reducing the need for volunteers, and around 80% of the turnover is self-funded. 'It was also important from the start to get funding from the participating village parish councils,' says Alan. 'It's not a fortune, but it's significant enough to cover operational funding, such as staff costs, and it shows they support the project.'

Turn over to discover how the Community Transport Association can help you set up a similar scheme.

£6 BILLION

The amount generated for rural communities every year through visits to National Parks*

FIND SUPPORT

The Community Transport Association (CTA) represents thousands of charities and community groups across the UK that provide transport services. Its general online FAQ section for operators of minibuses (9-16 passenger seats), or multi-purpose vehicles (less than 9) covers issues such as:
- **Driver licence checks**
- **Operator licences**
- **Safety inspections**
- **Traffic regulations**

THE NEXT STEP...
For more details on education and safety training, go to ctauk.org

operate a six-day-a-week bus service that offer journeys within an area of 12 miles, providing the journey is not already covered by a commercial bus service. Similarly, Bwcabus DRT in Wales, developed in partnership with three local authorities – Carmarthenshire, Pembrokeshire and Ceredigion – offers passengers the chance to travel where and when they want on pre-booked, demand-responsive journeys. These are booked through a call centre and are on a first-come-first-served basis.

Getting app happy

Campaign for National Parks has been campaigning rigorously to improve car-free access to parks around England and Wales, not just to improve affordable transport links for all, but to protect vulnerable landscape and wildlife. Visitors to National Parks play a huge role in supporting thousands of rural jobs in tourism.

One of the recommendations to come from its latest research is for funding from the Westminster government and/or the Welsh government for a 'smarter travel National Park' pilot to test new types of on-demand, app-based shared services, not unlike Vamooz. An app-based crowdfunding travel scheme, Vamooz allows users to nominate a journey for one of their buses (ie, a day trip to a National Park) then, quite simply, the more people who sign up to it, the lower the price becomes.

*Campaign for National Parks

LIFTING THE COMMUNITY

In Sedlescombe, East Sussex, a volunteer car service has been a lifeline for villagers travelling to medical appointments, particularly those who don't qualify for non-emergency patient transport.

Sometimes it's not necessarily a grant that a village needs – it's just a good idea and someone to make it happen. When Pauline Glew spotted a woman in tears in the street because there was no bus or taxi available to take her to a medical appointment, Pauline decided to act. 'The bus is every two hours into Hastings,' she says, 'plus there's no direct bus to the hospital or into Battle. I'd been a parish councillor for years, so I sat down with the clerk and came up with a simple scheme.

'Under the umbrella of the parish council, we now have a list of 12 drivers. One copy is held in the GP's surgery and I hold the other. When someone needs a lift to an appointment, they call an available driver from the list and pay a small charge to cover petrol. It's cheaper than the local taxi and more frequent than the buses. I even told East Sussex Healthcare NHS Trust about the scheme and they gave us 12 parking passes, one for each driver, so they don't have to pay when they do a drop-off or pick-up!' Sedlescombe's advice for setting up a similar scheme is...

- **Make sure drivers tell their insurance companies** about the scheme although, in Sedlescombe's experience, no one has had an issue with it.
- **Check the tax-free threshold for petrol expenses** (currently 45p per mile for the first 10,000 miles in the tax year). Go to gov.uk and type 'mileage payments as a volunteer driver' in the search bar.
- **Give each of your scheme drivers a lanyard** for easy identification.

GOING ELECTRIC

With the closure of petrol stations, many people living in rural areas may have to drive further to refuel. So could electric vehicles help? The Warwickshire Rural Electric Vehicle Trial, funded by Defra, supported 17 small and medium-sized businesses to lease electric vehicles from 2014-16. On the positive side, the businesses did report lower fuel costs. Feedback also focused on 'range anxiety' – the fear of running out of charge before the next charging point. Other negatives included a lack of charging points, an issue the National Infrastructure Commission highlighted last year when it estimated the cost of installing chargers at 200 currently unserved rural and remote areas would be around £10 million.

MAKING BUSINESS
WORK

Frustrated by a lack of job opportunities and the decline of the market town, many communities are creating their own business units – and brushing up their skills along the way

When The Prince's Countryside Fund commissioned its Recharging Rural research, 'poor variety of employment opportunities' was one of the top three barriers reported by people living in rural communities. Although, as one optimistic respondent put it: 'Entrepreneurs live everywhere, and our rural communities are alive with multi-talented, highly experienced business folk.'

The more 'rural' an area is, the higher the number of registered businesses per head of population*

S uccessful rural communities are underpinned by enterprise in many forms. So says Anna Price, director of The Rural Business Group, which works with commercial and community groups to support local economies. 'It may sound obvious, but it's vital to encourage businesses in your village,' she says. 'This can be anything from buying local produce and using local services (childcare providers, tradespeople), to encouraging the use of community spaces to support newly established businesses via hot desking and free wi-fi, or skills-sharing initiatives. Rural businesses often value community engagement above simply making a profit. They employ local people who might otherwise migrate and can provide valuable employment to people at the beginning or end of their working lives. It really is simple; think local and address challenges together – successful rural businesses mean better rural lives.'

Creating successful startups

As part of a project funded by The Prince's Countryside Fund, 40 independent rural startups have been receiving coaching from the Northumberland Community Development Company (NCDC). Called Back of Beyond Business Support, it offers workshops and networking, and supports farm-diversification businesses and young people. Louise Northwood is the project lead. 'About 85% of our startups are people currently working and looking to start a business on top,' she says. 'With such a big area

THE NEXT STEP...
Discover more at
ncdc.org.uk

*assets.publishing.service.gov.uk

HOW TO SET UP A BUSINESS HUB

Louise Northwood from the Northumberland Community Development Company shares her tips

1 **Form a steering group of volunteers or rural champions** and build relationships with all potential stakeholders in the area, as well as other existing supporters and funders. In our region, some of the organisations we worked with included The Prince's Countryside Fund, the Royal Agricultural Benevolent Institution and The Farming Community Network.

2 **Work out your costs in detail**, the biggest of which will inevitably be staffing. Budget for hidden costs, too, such as DBS checks and your insurance cover – both public liability and public indemnity.

3 **Spread the word about what you are doing** by joining local Facebook groups, creating interest via Twitter and building a link to your local newspaper.

4 **Pick your premises carefully** and think about disabled access and transport links. Is there parking and is it free? Are you on a bus or train route?

5 **Phone lines and superfast broadband are crucial**, but be aware that some of your infrastructure costs, such as your broadband provider, might tie you into a two-year contract. If your funding is only for 12 months, or the hub doesn't last, you will still be contracted. It might be cheaper to get a slightly more expensive provider on a one-year contract.

6 **Have at least two laptops** so that people can send emails and download forms and documents.

7 **Source training tools**, such as an overhead projector, if you can, and a whiteboard, so you have the potential to organise workshops. And collect leaflets, paperbacks and other resources to build a reference library.

8 **Take into account your lone worker policy** if there's only going to be one person at the hub. If possible, have two people, to safeguard both staff and the users.

9 **Provide a kettle and a comfy chair**, because sometimes people just want a friendly ear and a supportive chat.

10 **Ask local businesses for support**, they're often happy to help. In Hexham, the local accountants joined in with the book-keeping courses and shared their expert advice for free. As a result, they ended up gaining two new clients, so it was a win-win for everyone.

to cover, we're often limited to two or three visits a day, so the next step is to create a business hub. With office space, we can see more people and stretch the funds further.'

Another project helping businesses and startups is GROW South Antrim, which delivers funding under the Northern Ireland Rural Development Programme. This supports micro and small enterprises (under 50 full-time staff or equivalent), such as the joinery that received funds to buy new machinery; a move that should increase its production, boost sales and bring new job opportunities.

Expanding local markets

There's been a recent flurry of building activity at the Lochcarron Community Development Company (LCDC) in the Northwest Highlands. New funding, including grants from The Prince's Countryside Fund's Rural Four Project supported by players of People's Postcode Lottery, has enabled it to extend its existing building. The new space will have a café, kitchen, delicatessen counter and community space, and it's created five new full or part-time jobs.

The LCDC is also building on its support for local producers. Some already rent retail space on the site, plus there's a monthly market with 50 registered stallholders selling everything from jam and fudge, to fruit, vegetables and arts and crafts. And word of the market is spreading. 'We have half a dozen producers from a much wider area,' says local development officer Kristine MacKenzie. 'One bakery makes a 140-mile trip to sell its produce here!'

OPENING UP OPPORTUNITIES

'Previously, arts and crafts workers and local producers only had a single, once-a-month window to sell at the market or in our building. With the new development, we're giving them a permanent space where they can sell all year round and really increase their turnover.'
Kristine MacKenzie, LCDC

AIMING HIGH
Lochcarron's treehouse can host outdoor classrooms, workshops, or meetings, raising revenue for the community hub

IT'S ALL ABOUT THE SKILLS

With more a reliable digital infrastructure, people in rural areas have a better chance of setting up small local businesses or working from home.

Socially, home working means people are likely to be around the village more during the day, helping ease isolation for those unable to travel outside the community. But, unlike larger centralised workplaces, there are no IT help desks or 'techies' on hand to advise on apps, programs, how they work and what to do when they inevitably go wrong.

To help rural businesses harness digital technology and learn new skills, social-change charity Good Things Foundation worked with three training centres in Lincolnshire, North Yorkshire and Cumbria. During the three-year project, funded by The Prince's Countryside Fund, the centres supported 75 small and medium-sized rural businesses and organisations and 950 people.

Building on the success of the three-year initiative, Good Things Foundation is now engaged in a project to train up new digital champions across North and West Yorkshire with A1 Community Works and Airedale Enterprise Services.

Matt Moxon, the charity's digital inclusion officer, is in no doubt of the positive impact of the training.

'A lot of organisations have functioned perfectly well up to this point with paper invoices and a fax machine, but as different services, such as HMRC, become more digital, the need for better skills becomes more pressing,' he says. 'Some learners don't even know what they don't know, which is where training is so crucial. They may visit the centres asking for support in managing their tax return online, for instance, only for the trainers to discover that they have a limited knowledge of Microsoft Excel. So they can brush up on these skills as well and leave with much more than they came for.'

Small businesses with high digital capability are

2.5 TIMES

more likely to have an increase in turnover*

THE NEXT STEP... Discover more about digital champion training at goodthings foundation.org

*Lloyds Banking Group, Business Digital Index, 2017

IN OUR COMMUNITY
SHERSTON, WILTSHIRE

> ❛ Seven years on from launching our new business spaces, the old Victorian school premises have breathed new life into the high street and provide employment for more than 30 people ❜

When Sherston school relocated, leaving its prime location on the high street empty, a working group took action to 'stop the rot'. 'We set up the Sherston Old School Community Interest Company and attracted 280 residents as members and a board of volunteers selected for their skills, including an engineer and an accountant,' says Mike Johnson, chair of the Sherston Old School CIC.

'Phase one was to raise funds to buy and convert 40% of the space for the post office, at that time the only retail premises on the high street.'

They did this by, among other things, fundraising events, grants from Wiltshire Council and Sherston Parish Council and a Public Works Loan Board loan. Phase two, converting the rest of the premises into separate, small commercial units, was made possible by

more fundraising and a grant from The Prince's Countryside Fund.

In 2012, the old school opened six new business spaces, including a wine shop, a printer's and a software company (all previously run from home), and a design business that relocated from Malmesbury.

'We couldn't have done it without community support,' says Mike. 'And the parish council did a lot of early work as we wouldn't have been able to apply to the Public Works Loan Board without it.

'We've also been overpaying the rent for the site to build in some security. If a business were to drop out, we have a financial cushion to cover any big voids, although we've been fully occupied since opening – so far, so good!'

BOOSTING VISITOR FOOTFALL

When one national tourism enterprise expanded into a small Welsh community, they discovered benefits for both sides.

Tourism can be precariously seasonal, especially in remote areas, but one organisation bringing visitors to rural North Wales 365 days a year is Forest Holidays. With 10 locations on Forestry Commission land, from Scotland to Cornwall, the company offers premium cabins in woodland settings, with a small shop for essentials and a forest ranger for outdoor workshops. Other than that, the company ethos is to encourage its visitors to get out and about, to explore the area and all its amenities – and spend money in the community. This was a boost for the village of Beddgelert in Snowdonia National Park, a community of around 450 people and the site of the company's newest 16-cabin location.

Working together

There was initial nervousness among local businesses in Beddgelert that the new site would impact trade, but a year spent consulting with the community beforehand, including open days and coffee mornings to explain the vision, helped to reassure them.

Forest Holidays now heavily promotes many local businesses, with recommendations and visitor guides, and works with others to arrange special offers for its guests at local pubs, restaurants and attractions. It has been estimated that the amount guests at Beddgelert will contribute to the local economy could be as much as £500,000 annually.

There are also the obvious employment benefits that come with the new holiday development. Whereas some local people traditionally struggled to find year-round jobs in the locality, the new site now has 22 full-time staff, many of whom live locally.

COMMUNITY AND COMMERCE HAND IN HAND

Forest Holidays engages with the community at Beddgelert on many levels by...

1 Turning the location into a community hub for villagers with events at Bonfire Night, Halloween and Christmas.

2 Stocking local produce, such as fresh farm eggs, in the on-site shop.

3 Commissioning a local artist to create the paintings in the cabins and stocking the artwork in the shop.

4 Inviting people from local businesses to join in their staff first-aid training sessions.

5 Arranging school visits for outdoor sessions with the forest ranger and making educational visits to the school.

KEEPING IN
TOUCH

Good digital connections offer
increased business, employment
and social opportunities, which is
why many communities are getting
involved with projects to help shape
their own technology capabilities

Rural people are looking for a 'bright future of digital possibilities'. That was one of the conclusions from the Recharging Rural report commissioned by The Prince's Countryside Fund – as a result, communities are finding ways to bring broadband and digital opportunities to their residents.

Communities in the countryside need reliable, high-speed broadband and universal mobile coverage to support freelance working and to attract businesses to their area. But *need* and *have* are two very different things. In December 2018, Ofcom launched a campaign to help everyone understand their needs at boostyourbroadband.com. The campaign is also a way of checking availability in your area and discovering if you're paying too much. Yet picking your package is only relevant if the physical infrastructure is already in place.

Where connections aren't moving fast enough, some communities are making things happen for themselves. One group, 4CG, set up a co-operative to help the regeneration of Cardigan that included a wi-fi service allowing easy internet access on a pay-as-you-go basis. The 4CG wi-fi 'net' uses a new superfast-broadband connection to provide residents and visitors with good browsing speeds, without the need for subscriptions, installing a phone line or a contract. Yet with EE's launch in May 2019 of the UK's first 5G service in six cities, it's clear that rural areas still without 4G provision are likely to fall further behind in the connectivity stakes.

33%
The proportion of rural buildings where it's impossible to make a basic call on the four mobile networks (EE, Three, O2 and Vodafone)*

Inspired to use spires
Around 65% of Anglican churches in England are in rural parishes, so it's no surprise that an accord was signed in 2018 to encourage the Church of England to use its churches to boost broadband, mobile and wi-fi connections for their communities. Since the agreement, between the National Church Institutions of the Church of England, the Department for Digital, Culture, Media & Sport (DCMS) and the Department for Environment Food &

The State of Rural Services Report/Rural England CIC

Rural Affairs (Defra), was signed, more than 30 churches have started work on projects and dozens more are pending. Not that the idea was new. Throughout Norfolk, broadband service provider WiSpire began using spires and church towers, such as All Saints Wreningham (above), to improve connectivity back in 2011.

'Churches are often the tallest structures in a village, so can be perfect for those who are tucked away in areas where traditional, slower broadband is expensive, or just not fast enough,' says Brandon March from InTouch Systems, which took over WiSpire's business in 2018. 'When installing our equipment, we're careful to preserve the structures. These are important historical landmarks and often older buildings. To minimise visibility of our equipment from the spires and peaks, we use a scaffolding rig which rests on top of the church, as opposed to drilling and screwing, so that no damage is done to the building.'

Where there's a will, there's wi-fi

One community familiar with the pitfalls of trying to get connected is the Wereham Village Hall charity in Norfolk. It opened its new village hall in 2018, but all was not plain sailing in the technology department.

'Underestimate the difficulty of getting connected to the phone and internet at your peril,' says Victoria Gray, chair of the management committee. 'We put the connection request in during construction of the building and, a year later, we still didn't have a connection date. To

THINKING OUTSIDE THE BOX

Broadband in a Box is a series of guides and policies that any small, rural-based group can use to develop its own broadband solutions. It was produced by Cybermoor – which has been working to improve digital connectivity in the Alston Moor area of Cumbria since 2001 – following on from its own experience of delivering the Broadband Delivery UK (BDUK) pilot in 2016.

THE NEXT STEP
Find out more at
cybermoor.org

bypass that, we found out which mobile company had the best wi-fi reception in our area (most providers allow you to check 4G coverage by postcode) and found that EE was best for us. So we bought a mobile broadband device for around £30 a month, which gives 15GB of data. This is more than sufficient to run the staff laptops, but the signal was struggling to support a weekly IT course provided by Norfolk Community Learning Service (NCLS). To resolve that, NCLS provided two wi-fi access points to boost the signal strength and it worked really well.'

Making connections

In May 2019, the DCMS announced an update to its £67 million Gigabit Broadband Voucher Scheme, part of its Local Full Fibre Networks programme. Small businesses can apply for vouchers, currently up to £3,500, to use towards the installation cost of a gigabit-capable connection, for fast, reliable broadband. Vouchers of up to £1,500 are also available to residents. These vouchers, or grants, can be used in conjunction with the Openreach Community Fibre Partnerships initiative that works with communities to find solutions to connectivity problems. Openreach covers the costs in line with its commercial model and the community funds anything on top of that. If communities aren't included in Openreach fibre roll-out plans, in Broadband Delivery UK (BDUK) plans, or if they're too far away from a fibre cabinet, Community Fibre Partnership could offer a solution.

The CLA, the membership organisation for owners of land, property and business in rural England and Wales, says communities are looking for new ways to get connected. These include business owners investing in their own broadband connection, such as fibre-to-premises, then becoming local suppliers using local wi-fi networks.

Technical innovation for Cornwall

Vodafone recently announced an initiative to improve mobile coverage in rural areas using disused BT phone boxes. One idea is to install 4G technology in beachfront phone boxes, boosting reception for a 200-yard radius. The pilots are in the Cornish resorts of Polzeath and Sennen Cove and it's hoped they will help cope with the increase in mobile usage during the summer.

1 IN 5

rural businesses is having to make its own investments to get connected*

THE NEXT STEP
Find out more at gigabitvoucher. culture.gov.uk, scotlandsuperfast. com, gov.wales/ go-superfast and communityfibre. openreach.co.uk

*cla.org.uk

HOW TO SET UP COMMUNITY BROADBAND

1 Check the level of service provision in your area at gosuperfastchecker. culture.gov.uk

2 Form an action group or use an existing platform such as the parish council to discuss your community's needs. This includes nominating a local leader and deciding on a legal structure, ie, do you want to become a social enterprise?

3 Establish the size of the area involved and the population density.

4 Engage with local stakeholders such as landowners who might need to grant access to their land, local businesses that might be willing to co-fund, and the local body/ council for information on planned infrastructure upgrades in your community.

5 Explore the best options for your community, such as approaching a supplier directly, buying into an existing commercial rollout, buying into a publicly funded rollout, or more.

6 Consider raising funds as a community, or by pooling voucher schemes such as the Gigabit Broadband Voucher Scheme from the DCMS.

7 Check out suppliers in your region that may be able to provide improved broadband connectivity through the Better Broadband Scheme.

8 For guidance on getting started, registered suppliers and case studies go to gov.uk and type 'community-led broadband' into the search bar.

IN OUR COMMUNITY
CUMBRIA, LANCASHIRE & YORKSHIRE

‘ When we started out, everything was done by volunteers. Now the company employs 30 people, so it's a great example of a business that's flourished in the seven years it's been running ’

Internet service provider B4RN (Broadband for the Rural North) is an affordable fibre-optic broadband network bringing communities online in North Lancashire, North Yorkshire and Cumbria. Each new area has to raise investment to cover the work and materials via shares and, once the infrastructure is in place, users pay a one-off connection charge and a monthly fee.

Ian Thompson joined B4RN as a volunteer in order to connect the houses in his community, but caught the bug and likes nothing better than to be at the bottom of a muddy hole! He has been a director since 2016.

'I lived in a converted farm and there were 12 households,' he says. 'It was the archetypal B4RN target – in the middle of nowhere, agricultural and easy to reach once we had the landowner's

agreement to dig. I was a new arrival who didn't know anyone but, as a result of this project I got to know them well. I had so much fun, that five years later I'm still volunteering.

'We're a limited company with shares bought by people in the community. People are prepared to not only put in the effort, but also their own money.

'Technically, the system is brilliant, but socially it has an impact far beyond that. One volunteer wrote to everyone who helped his house get connected, saying "I'd like you to understand the difference this has made. It is now 8pm and all my children have finished their homework. Until now they had to take turns using the internet and the last one couldn't finish until midnight!"'

TIME TO NETWORK

Good, sustainable digital links are crucial to rural communities, but technology alone can't alleviate the feelings of isolation. Finding other ways to join the community dots requires action from local residents.

S etting up a local network via Facebook is one way to connect people, covering everything from items for sale, to publicising events or even setting up a Past, Present, Future theme where people can share memories and old photos. Or you could establish a network like Nextdoor. There are currently more than 15,000 Nextdoor neighbourhoods and it's relatively easy to start one up. Your Nextdoor group can be used for finding lost pets, searching for tradespeople and reporting updates on road works, or helping in emergencies, including severe weather and flooding. Groups also work with police forces and local authorities that have a dedicated platform on Nextdoor, allowing them to engage directly with residents. In Northern Ireland, it helped one blind runner find a running guide to help him get fit, while in Pluckley, Kent, it revitalised the Neighbourhood Watch scheme co-ordinated by Martin Chambers.

Martin had been trying to grow membership, but it was a slow climb. It had taken him nearly three years to get the Facebook group up to 80 and the email group up to 200. But once he'd posted on Nextdoor, it was soon up to 350, almost 50% of the village. 'It's turned Neighbourhood Watch on its head,' he says. 'Residents are now posting their own alerts and others are responding. It's amazing really, because it's all about awareness, and about people knowing what is happening down their street.'

90%

of the country has a Nextdoor group recommending tradespeople, reporting local news and making connections in the community

HOW TO GET
HELP
WHEN YOU
NEED IT

From extreme weather to
medical emergencies, everyone
needs support at certain times in
their life. It's not always easy to
deliver in rural areas, but plenty of
communities are finding ways with
their own resilience plans

Floods, storms and power failures can cause havoc anywhere – in rural locations it can be devastating. When remote communities are challenged with emergencies of any kind, help can feel a long way off, which is why planning ahead is so crucial.

A s many rural communities have found to their cost, extreme weather, such as severe gales or flooding can leave them vulnerable and isolated. The Prince's Countryside Fund has an emergency fund which is available if and when it's needed. It can also launch appeals to gather personal and corporate donations. Increasingly, however, communities have been focusing on resilience planning to help mitigate the damage these events can inflict.

SOUNDS LIKE A PLAN...
'We've created a telephone tree of people who could turn out in an emergency, to help clear roads, or make sure those who can't get out are looked after'
Ian Papworth, Trelawnyd Community Association

You've got the power

The communities of Trelawnyd and Gwaenysgor in North Wales often suffer power failures and find themselves cut off during bad weather. Determined to discover ways around this, the community councils for the two villages drew up a resilience plan that identified the need for two new generators. 'We thought if we could equip our village halls with a generator each, plus an emergency box (with things such as plastic gloves, hi-vis vests and plastic thermal blankets like you see at the end of a marathon), they could become emergency rest centres,' says Ian Papworth, secretary of the Trelawnyd Community Association. 'We've also created a telephone tree of people who could turn out in an emergency, to help clear roads, or make sure those who can't get out are looked after, so it's another way of bringing a village together.'

The main contacts on the emergency list are the chair and vice chair of the community council – both of them have a list of people to call out, such as farming families with equipment like low-loader trailers, tractors and four-wheel drives. 'It's all about making sure we can keep going till the county snowplough arrives, or the power comes back on,' says Ian. 'We just asked people if they

HOW TO CREATE YOUR OWN COMMUNITY EMERGENCY PLAN

WHY MIGHT WE NEED ONE?

- A plan helps a community cope on its own if emergency services are not immediately available, BUT it's not the role of the community to take on the responsibilities of these agencies or to take risks.
- A plan lets people know what they can do in advance to reduce risks and be prepared.
- A plan helps communications within the community and with statutory bodies, linking up local-knowledge facilities and people.

WHO LEADS IT?

You'll need a small steering group to create the plan and a community response group (CRG) to co-ordinate its delivery. These two groups could be the same people, but they don't necessarily have to be.

WHAT MIGHT IT INCLUDE?

- Contact details of the community response group.
- Triggers that would activate the plan, such as extreme snow and ice, flooding, storms and gales, moorland fires, or power failure.
- Contact details of community resources and how they could help.
- Key contacts for the authorities and emergency services.
- A risk assessment for volunteers, including what safety procedures are already in place and what else could be done to control risks.

HOW DO WE SET IT UP?

- Liaise with local authorities, your rural community council (if you have one) and emergency services, so they know what you're doing and can help where possible.
- Talk to residents and businesses, including farmers, to find out what resources are available, such as skills, facilities, equipment and potential volunteers.
- Assess who in the community might be at greater risk or harder to contact.
- Nominate a 'place of safety', such as the village hall, which could provide shelter and access to information or supplies.

were willing to help and what kit they would have available, which also meant we didn't have to spend a great deal on equipment.'

The generators, funded by The Prince's Countryside Fund, are in the community halls of both villages and have a value that goes way beyond crisis management. 'Resilience is also about community cohesion, so for outside events, such as our carnival, we now have an extra generator,' says Ian. 'The spin off from working with the other village is that we all know each other now. Before we just knew *of* each other.'

Planning at all levels

Someone else who believes in the value of planning is Lorrainne Smyth, chief executive of ACTion with Communities in Cumbria, although she believes that this doesn't necessarily always have to be a large-scale resilience plan co-ordinated by a committee.

'After Storm Desmond, local authorities were keen for all communities and buildings to have a plan in place, which was a significant challenge given that nearly 60,000 buildings were flooded,' she says. 'We decided to think about it in a slightly different way. With a project funded by The Prince's Countryside Fund, we worked with around 300 village halls, encouraging them to consider their risks. It's all about having the conversation and getting people to think about their own circumstances.

'In one village, their recurring emergency is the closing of the M66 for snow, so they got some funding to put in a couple of camp beds, with things like sleeping bags and towels. Now, when people can't get through the blocked roads, they can offer them somewhere to stay. It's a solution that's very specific to them, but it doesn't take much to put together, and they feel good about themselves. Things like this make people more likely to help each other in an emergency.

'We also encourage people to take a more neighbourly approach by drawing up a household plan, which is another part of our online managing-risk toolkit. You don't need a formal document for this; it's more about people working together. If the electricity is out and you have gas, for instance, you can cook for people, take them a cuppa, or invite them in. Even the smallest gestures help.'

341.4

During Storm Desmond in 2015, Honister in Cumbria had 341.4mm of rain in 24 hours, breaking all previous UK records*

THE NEXT STEP... For more information and templates for resilience planning, go to cumbriaaction.org.uk

*The Met Office

IN OUR COMMUNITY
APPLEBY, CUMBRIA

> ❛ Although many residents watch flood warnings on the Environment Agency website, or have signed up for alerts, some older people who don't use technology rely on hearing a siren ❜

The residents of Appleby, Cumbria, are all too familiar with flooding. In December 2015, the River Eden burst its banks three times in one month, flooding around 40 properties and causing thousands of pounds worth of damage. But the upheaval caused was incalculable, which was why Appleby fundraised for a new flood siren.

'Traditionally, people responded unofficially to flood situations by knocking on doors to check on others, but it was made formal in 2016 when the Appleby Emergency Response Group became official, with a management committee and a constitution,' says Keira Booth, the group's project manager.

With donations left from well-wishers after

Storm Desmond and funding from the Cumbria Community Foundation, the group was able to pay for things such as a laptop, volunteer training and a funded manager. And it was soon clear the old, manually operated siren that dated back to WWII needed replacing.

Last summer, a grant of £12,000 from The Prince's Countryside Fund paid for a new, remotely operated siren, now in place on the side of the rebuilt cricket pavilion,

more centrally located than the previous siren.

'Flooding will always be the main emergency here, so moving forward we'd like to focus on any prevention measures the Environment Agency is considering,' says Keira.

'For any project, try to start local and build relationships – our district council couldn't have been more helpful. There are people out there whose job it is to support community groups, but you don't always know they're there!'

BEING PREPARED

Some of the ways for villages to become more resilient may be as simple as boosting first-aid knowledge, or by encouraging people to become Community First Responders (CFRs).

CFRs are teams of volunteers trained by their local Ambulance Service to be first on the scene in their own community. And in hard-to-reach areas they can, quite literally, be life-savers. Most carry basic equipment, such as oxygen, and their task is to help stabilise the patient until ambulance crews arrive. East Midlands Ambulance Service, for instance, has around 800 CFRs that responded to 32,000 emergency calls in 2018 in Leicestershire, Northamptonshire, Derbyshire, Nottinghamshire and Rutland (a separate charity called LIVES manages CFRs across Lincolnshire).

Initial training is an intensive three-day course and volunteers are asked to commit to being on call for a minimum of 200 hours a year, so that they utilise their skills regularly, although most far exceed that amount, booking on for around 400-500 hours per year.

Building skills and resources

You don't have to be a firefighter to use a fire extinguisher and you don't have to be a paramedic to use a defibrillator – that's the message from the Community Heartbeat Trust (CHT), a charity which supports communities that want to acquire, install and maintain a defibrillator.

'There's no legal requirement to train users, but we believe training is important, not just in how to use the equipment, but also how to spot someone in cardiac arrest, do CPR correctly and how to make a 999 call,' says CHT secretary Martin Fagan.

CHT also came up with the idea of using old phone kiosks for defibrillators and now has around 1,000 kiosk

'State of Rural Services report/February 2019

Photography: Emily Snow

FIRST ON THE SCENE
Trent District Community First Responders work in partnership with East Midlands Ambulance Service

sites. 'It's not just about defibrillators,' says Martin. 'About six years ago, we were working with BT and North West Ambulance Service, putting defibrillators into old kiosks, but the Lake District National Park was worried about closing them all down because they were keen to maintain a 999 function. So we suggested installing pre-programmed emergency phones, which are basically buttons that look a bit like intercoms instead. Most have been installed beside defibrillators in phone boxes, but they don't have to be. We can put them anywhere as a standalone, such as on the side of a village hall.'

30%
of rural residents live more than 30 minutes' drive from a major hospital*

Putting first aid first

Knowledge of first aid is an obvious benefit to rural communities, especially if that training includes skills specific to remote areas. In 2015, a Northern Ireland Farm Safety Partnership survey suggested that up to 100 accidents requiring some form of medical attention occurred every month on farms in Northern Ireland. This prompted the College of Agriculture, Food & Rural Enterprise (CAFRE) to launch its Farm Family Key Skills First Aid workshops. To date, more than 1,500 people associated with farm businesses have attended 88 of the three-hour courses held across local venues in Northern Ireland. Topics on the courses include common on-farm risks, dangers and injuries; practical steps and CPR; and the tools and technologies that could aid lone workers in an emergency.

THE NEXT STEP...
For more information on Farm Family Key Skills courses, go to cafre.ac.uk

SHARING THE CARING
Getting help when you need it isn't just about life-threatening situations, it's often about ongoing social-care needs.

20%

In some rural counties, over 20% of the population is more than 65 years old*

Supported by a grant from The Prince's Countryside Fund, the Bell View Reaching Out project addresses rural and social isolation in Northumberland by bringing people together to create hubs in community venues. The sessions provide nutritious food and are facilitated by care workers as well as volunteers to ensure that those with mobility or care needs aren't excluded. As well as the social events, the four staff and 40 volunteers run over 150 trips a month to help people get to doctor's appointments, do shopping, or meet friends.

For one 87-year-old widow, the service is a lifeline. 'This lady lives in a very remote cottage, a few miles from the village and doesn't have any transport,' says Jane Field, Bell View's services development manager. 'Although she gets lonely, she's fiercely independent and reluctant to ask for help for what she sees as trivial things, such as getting out for a coffee. We run coffee mornings and soup-and-sandwich lunches in the village hall nearest to where she lives and, as we were offering transport, she agreed to come along.'

Since engaging with Bell View, the lady has met up with people from the bowls team, which she used to enjoy with her husband, and has been on assisted shopping trips. 'We know she feels reconnected with the village again, because she tells us, "When my daughter rings to see how I am, now I have something to talk about"!'

Who cares? We care...
Julia Darby is executive director of community-owned care provider NEDCare CIC in the North East Dartmoor area. 'In 2014, after the closure of the cottage hospital in Moretonhampstead, which acted as a staging post between acute patients coming out of hospital and going

THE NEXT STEP...
Read the report 'Issues Facing Providers of Social Care at Home to Older Rural Residents' at ruralengland.org

*ruralengland.org

back to the community, a group of local people formed a working group,' she explains. 'With a little funding from the then Department for Communities and Local Government, we consulted with the community and county council and found that the area was described as being in "market failure" for social care. Effectively, it meant there were no providers the local authority could buy regulated care from.'

The group knew they had to set up a regulated agency to meet local needs, but also knew that would take a lot of time and startup funding – around £80,000. With a grant from Moretonhampstead Hospital League of Friends, they first set up a Carer Introduction Service and built up a database of around 40 self-employed carers, putting them in touch with people with care needs.

'It was a quick, cheap and effective way of proving we were making an impact and meeting needs,' says Julia. 'So when we started crowdfunding for the regulated business, everyone knew about the project and supported us. We were entirely set up by the local community.'

NEDCare CIC was regulated in 2017 so it can no longer use self-employed carers. It now directly employs 20 carers and delivers 700 hours of regulated care a month over an area of about 250 square miles. 'Setting up the introduction service was a great stepping stone to starting the regulated company,' says Julia. 'Other communities have been in touch to ask how we did it, and we've had some funding from Transform Ageing to produce a toolkit, which will be ready this summer, for anyone interested in setting up an introductory service.'

MOVING FORWARD
'The thought of having to register with the Care Quality Commission and all the regulations that involved was more psychologically challenging in the anticipation of it than it was in the doing. Once we started, it was fine!'
Julia Darby, NEDCare

CLEANING UP
NEDCare promoting its bathing services in Devon

WHERE TO FIND
FUNDING

You've got the vision, the plan,
the motivation and a team of
volunteers just raring to go...
The big hurdle to any community
project can be finding the money
to make it happen

Although the options can be a little overwhelming, when it comes to funding there's lots of associations and networks out there to give you support and confidence – not to mention other communities that can share their experiences.

£10 MILLION

The amount The Prince's Countryside Fund has given to more than 250 projects in the UK since 2010

I n recent years, public funding for rural development projects has come from a wide range of short-term funding pots, distributed by the four governments of the UK. Rural communities have also benefited from EU funding through a range of initiatives and schemes distributed through LEADER. While we wait for confirmation on the UK's Shared Prosperity Fund, and what this may mean for rural communities, groups will have to secure funding from a wide range of individuals, schemes and loans. Here are just some of the organisations that can help you through the application process.

- **Plunkett Foundation** Currently supporting over 400 communities, the Plunkett Foundation helps groups across the UK set up a community business with practical advice, support, training, tools, resources and networking events. *plunkett.co.uk*
- **Pub is The Hub** A not-for-profit organisation that helps communities looking to introduce or reopen services or activities in their local pub. *pubisthehub.org.uk*
- **Locality** The national membership network for community organisations with over 600 Locality members across England. *locality.org.uk*
- The community-led regeneration and enterprise networks of the **Development Trusts Association Wales, Development Trusts Assocation Scotland** and **Development Trusts NI**. *dtawales.org.uk; dtascot.org.uk; dtni.org.uk*
- **The National Lottery Community Fund** (formerly the Big Lottery Fund) distributes over £600 million a year to communities across the UK, raised by players of The National Lottery. *tnlcommunityfund.org.uk*
- **Local councils and rural development organisations** such as ACRE (Action with Communities in Rural England). *acre.org.uk*

5 WAYS TO FIND FUNDING

1 Donations and fundraising

Often the first step in any project, this is all about fetes raffles, auctions and musical events. It's time consuming, but fun, and a way to spread the message, raise awareness and engage local businesses.

Bear in mind… It's unlikely to raise the level of money that many projects need to buy premises or start community businesses, but it often helps secure a 'fighting fund' to pay for surveys, legal documents, printing or publicity.

2 Community shares

Another effective way to raise substantial amounts is through a community share offer. If your group has become a not-for-profit organisation, such as a co-operative society, or a community benefit society (CBS), you can generate funding by drawing up a share offer document to deliver your community project. Under the CBS model, each shareholder has one vote, irrespective of the number of shares they have bought.

Bear in mind… Minimum share investment in a CBS could be as little as £1. The statutory maximum by one individual or company is £100,000, although the Plunkett Foundation recommends a CBS sets its own maximum investment at an appropriate level to avoid individuals having undue influence.

HOW WE DID IT…

When The New Inn Pub in Norton Lindsey, Warwickshire, closed in July 2016, it was already registered as an asset of community value. A group of locals called the Salvation Squad formed a community benefit society and set out to buy it. The pub reopened in April 2017. They did it with the help of…

- **£2,500** bursary from the Plunkett Foundation's More Than A Pub scheme.
- **£500** grant towards a 'fighting fund' from Norton Lindsey Parish Council.
- **£324,000** from 226 shareholders in a community share issue.
- **£50,000** loan and a **£50,000** grant from More Than A Pub's key fund.
- There were also grants from Pub is The Hub and Warwick District Council, which were ringfenced to create a small local shop.

Photography: Robin Woolgar Photography

To stop their historic pub, the Duke of Marlborough, being converted to housing and lost forever, the village of Somersham in Suffolk started a Save the Duke campaign.

- With advice from the Plunkett Foundation and other pubs – many community-owned – they formed a community benefit society in 2015.
- They offered shares via Crowdfunder UK with a minimum investment of £250, which comprised five shares at £50 each.
- In November 2015, the society successfully raised £183,570 through 167 investors in 75 days.
- They also received a combined grant and loan from the Plunkett Foundation's More Than A Pub project.
- The community-owned pub re-opened in summer 2017.

3 Grants

These can range from hundreds of thousands to a few hundred pounds, and they're often available through local councils, including the local authority and current government schemes, so start your search locally. You can also apply via national charities such as The National Lottery Community Fund, The Prince's Countryside Fund, People's Postcode Lottery, or the Esmée Fairbairn Foundation. Grants are rarely given upfront, so you'll be expected to raise startup money. And grants aren't limited to community groups, charities and social enterprises – they can be available for private businesses like pubs working with local authorities to provide community services such as a mini library or a digital hub.

Bear in mind... Grants require a business plan, including evidence of long-term sustainability, and a contingency plan in case you are not awarded the full amount.

4 Crowdfunding

One way of raising funds quickly and testing local support for a project is via crowdfunding, which is essentially collecting (usually) small amounts of money from a wide range of people using an online platform such as spacehive.com, crowdfunder.co.uk, or ukcfa.org.uk. It can be a good way to raise matched funds from grant-givers and it shows community support to other funders.

Bear in mind... If you don't reach the total amount you set as a target, you cannot draw down the money already pledged, which can dilute the project's momentum.

5 Loans

A number of approved loan providers called Community Development Finance Institutions (CDFIs) lend exclusively to community-owned enterprises and social enterprises. Another potential source of affordable borrowing is via the Public Works Loan Board (PWLB). A community business or social enterprise is unable to apply to the PWLB, but a parish council can. It can then make money available to a project in the form of a grant. Discover more at nalc.gov.uk and dmo.gov.uk

Bear in mind... Securing a loan can show your business plan is creditworthy, but it has to be paid back, so this must be factored into turnover and income requirements.

IN OUR COMMUNITY
BANTON, NORTH LANARKSHIRE

> ❝ It's been an interesting journey becoming the first community-owned pub in Scotland. There were times when things lined up brilliantly and others when we thought – what have we started? ❞

When the future of the Swan Inn looked to be in jeopardy in 2016, the village of Banton formed People United for Banton and set out to buy it. 'We'd lost our shop and post office, and the bus services had been cut, so we were in danger of becoming a commuter zone not a village,' says the group's vice chair, Catherine Moneypenny.

Once they started applying for funding, the Scottish Land Fund and Big Lottery Community Assets paid for feasibility studies and the Plunkett Foundation helped with legal advice. The first big grant from the Scottish Land Fund was £184,000, 95% of the cost of buying the pub; the second wave included £740,000 from the Big Lottery Fund and support from the Kelvin Valley & Falkirk LEADER Programme.

'With the money in place, we went out to tender and hit a brick wall,' says Catherine. 'It came back significantly higher than expected. It was like landing on the last snake in snakes and ladders! We had to look for funding again. The Clothworkers' Foundation gave us a grant and the final piece of the jigsaw fell into place when we were told we could register for VAT and claim back around the same amount we were short.'

Construction will start in the summer of 2019 after which People United for Banton will launch a share offer with support from Community Shares Support Scotland and an advisor (funded by The Prince's Countryside Fund via the Plunkett Foundation).

'Even before work has started the impact on the village has been fantastic,' says Catherine, 'with over a third of villagers volunteering their time to the project.'

Photography: Light of Louise Photography

WHAT DOES THE

FUTURE

HOLD?

No one can be certain... But what
we do know is that sustainable,
resilient villages will be those
that have access to broadband
and mobile phone coverage,
embrace innovation, engage young
people and explore the amazing
opportunities their village already
offers – its assets and its people

While rural communities will continue to face many challenges – both old and new – there are brighter possibilities ahead.

The Prince's Countryside Fund was launched in 2010 to help improve the viability of rural communities. Through working with its partners and funding over 250 practical and innovative projects, the charity has become increasingly aware that the issues affecting our rural communities could continue to be complex and challenging without three things – the ongoing creativity and vigour of villagers, effective collaboration with local stakeholders, and investment and support through the UK's Shared Prosperity Fund.

In April 2019, a House of Lords Select Committee published its report 'Time for a strategy for the rural community', highlighting key challenges. These included declining farm profitability, Brexit, an ageing population, climate change and the pressure from often piecemeal and inappropriate development. 'The Lords Report suggests a rural strategy and rural proofing is needed on a Government level to underpin local, place-based activity,' says Claire Saunders, director of The Prince's Countryside Fund. This has also been called for by the Rural Business Network in its report 'Time for a Rural Strategy'.

WHAT IS THE UK'S SHARED PROSPERITY FUND?

The Government has pledged to set up a Shared Prosperity Fund to 'reduce inequalities in communities'. It is proposed to replace the structural funding received from the EU, which included the European Agriculture Fund for Rural Development.

We did it, so can you!

'Rural communities wish to be listened to, respected and understood.' That's the belief of Professor Sarah Skerratt, director of policy engagement at Scotland's Rural College, who worked closely with The Prince's Countryside Fund to analyse the findings. 'Individuals and communities have a breadth and depth of experience, wisdom and knowledge that they wish to share, both with other communities and with those creating policies that affect rural areas and businesses.'

Sharing achievements was a key message in Recharging Rural, which highlighted recommendations for policy makers, rural stakeholders and, crucially, for communities themselves. If one village can successfully reopen a shop through a community share issue, who better to inspire

OPEN FOR
BUSINESS
Cheriton Fitzpaine
Community Shop in
Devon – run by, and
for, the community

another village by passing on their experiences and
challenges? It echoes the message from the Smart Villages
initiative, part of the EU's European Network for Rural
Development, which defines Smart Villages as 'rural areas
and communities which build on their existing strengths
and assets as well as on developing new opportunities'.

Another key conclusion in Recharging Rural was for
communities to be imaginative with these assets, making
better use of new technologies, flexible, multi-use spaces,
mobile services and pop-ups. Many of the 550 projects
that responded had a strong focus on bringing people
together. The most common were community hubs,
providing a variety of services on a practical level, and on a
social level, too, helping to reduce isolation and loneliness.

All in it together

Community groups can't do everything alone, though.
Policymakers and groups providing practical support also
need to improve their understanding of, and respect for,
rural communities. As one respondent to Recharging
Rural put it: 'Some things can be – and are – addressed
locally by local people (if they can find funding), but many
other things require thought and action at government
level. No amount of local initiatives will change how
local authorities or the health service are funded.'

Imagination is also crucial if communities are to be
forward thinking and sustainable, says Rob Poole FRSA,
one of four 'animateurs' based in Cornwall, working

**PICKING UP
THE PACE**
'Compared to
previous years,
communities are
getting projects off
the ground much
sooner. They're
learning from the
trailblazers who
have gone before
and effectively
fast-tracking
through the process,
particularly where
fundraising is
concerned. Groups
are much better
now at asking for
help and support'
*Sarah Lee, head
of policy at the
Countryside Alliance*

Photography: Ian Southerin

WHAT IS AN ANIMATEUR?

Someone who engages and leads sustainable strategies in village settings 'from the bottom up'. Animateurs encourage decision-making at a local level with the aim of creating more flexible and innovative responses to local problems.

on projects in fishing villages across the UK. 'We don't signpost, we don't facilitate, we sit down and fill in forms with people, taking them through complex government-speak and making it happen,' he says. 'What we do as animateurs is very transferable, but you need a culture that will accept change. Communities need to understand that the risk is worth taking. Not financial risk, but project risk.'

Passing on the baton is also vital. As community leaders get older or suffer 'burnout', communities need to plan their leadership succession carefully to ensure there's a new wave of people coming through which is willing to inspire collaboration and keep the momentum going. It's also important to consider the skills needed at different stages in a project – from planning and building to running a successful, viable business – and to identify who can offer those particular skills.

Trends to watch

So what might be on the horizon for rural communities?

- **Better connectivity?** There's no doubt that better broadband and mobile infrastructure has the potential to transform the rural economy, opening up more opportunities for home working and small business growth. And the government's investment in digital health, which offers an opportunity to improve access to health services in rural areas, is welcome.

  As the Smart Villages initiative concluded: 'Our rural communities need jobs, basic services, connectivity and smart transport solutions, as well

VOLUNTEERS WELCOME...

...at the Cilcain Community Shop and Café, Flintshire

as a favourable climate for entrepreneurship. We must enable new types of business models to emerge, such as portal-based services, and existing rural businesses to connect, integrate and co-operate better with urban-based businesses.'

- **Better opportunities for business?** If youth migration and access to affordable housing remains a challenge, then businesses may continue to face skills shortages. The availability of rural working spaces is also a key concern, particularly among small businesses looking to grow. Arts and the creative industries are following on from where tourism and on-farm diversification has led, although they also need good connectivity to be able to sell their products through social media and online marketplaces.

There's also great potential to continue strengthening the role that private businesses, such as pubs, can play by using their premises to offer community benefits, from GP drop-ins and libraries to digital hubs. Social enterprises and community-owned businesses and amenities will also continue to need support. Not just in relation to grant finance and bidding for service delivery contracts, but also for practical, impartial advice and guidance to help fulfil their potential.

- **Better fuel options?** Extreme weather events can hit rural communities hard and, with climate change, the need to adapt and use resources to reduce emissions is crucial. As Claire Saunders from The Prince's Countryside Fund says: 'Many people in rural communities are hit by fuel poverty, without access to mains gas supply, and are reliant on oil and wood for heating. This is why it's so important to invest in community renewable-energy schemes now, and to consider future needs, such as electric-car charging points, which will all be key factors in sustainability.'

LOOKING AHEAD

'While European business grants programmes like LEADER have an uncertain future, there are still national programmes aimed at improving digital connectivity and supporting community energy projects in some parts of the country. Influencing and understanding the rural component of the new national Shared Prosperity Fund, potentially starting in 2022, may help provide future solutions.'
Andy Walker, head of business growth, Lancashire Enterprise Partnership

MAKING THEIR VOICES HEARD

The Scottish Association of Young Farmers Clubs has more than 3,000 members under 30, who currently have a 'seat at the table' with external groups from Orkney to Westminster

THE NEXT STEP...

Follow the vloggers sharing the issues facing the young in rural areas at ruralyouthproject. com

Talking 'bout my generation

The conundrum of sustainable rural living is that the people who will deliver the future, the young, are increasingly moving away in search of affordable housing and job opportunities. The even bigger danger is that there's no opportunity for them to come back, to get on the property ladder, or to find suitable employment that they are skilled and qualified to do. That's why engaging them now – to pass on the legacy of community action – is key. The Rural Youth Project, launched in 2018, used an online survey to tap into the thoughts of young people aged 18-28 in several countries, including 570 from England, Scotland and Wales. Despite issues with housing, transport, connectivity and job opportunities, over 70% said they were optimistic about the future. On the down side, only 13% felt they had a say in their communities.

'Within the village context, there is a fear of older people not taking their views seriously,' says project director Rebecca Dawes. 'There didn't seem to be an understanding of how to improve that so, hopefully, we can boost the confidence of both. We have 10 UK-based vloggers sharing their experiences in rural communities, talking about their challenges, their careers and possible solutions. The project will continue until at least 2022 and young people are driving it, so we hope these conversations will help intergenerational understanding.'

Photography: Euan McCall

THANKS TO...

The Prince's Countryside Fund would like to thank the following for their advice, guidance and recommendations for The Village Survival Guide

- Action with Communities in Rural England (ACRE)
- Campaign for National Parks
- Campaign to Protect Rural England (CPRE)
- CLA
- Cornwall and Isles of Scilly Local Enterprise Partnership
- Cornwall Rural Community Charity
- Countryside Alliance
- Defra
- English Rural
- Good Things Foundation
- Locality
- Margaret Clark CBE
- National Associaton of Local Councils (CALC)
- Nick Mack
- PLANED
- Plunkett Foundation
- Professor Sarah Skerratt
- Pub is The Hub
- Rural Action NI
- Rural Housing Scotland
- Rural Services Network
- Rural Youth Project (Jane Craigie Marketing)

With special thanks to these organisations and groups which shared their first-hand experiences

- ACTion with Communities in Cumbria
- Appleby Emergency Response Group, Cumbria
- B4RN (Broadband for the Rural North)
- Bamford Community Society, Peak District
- Bell View, Northumberland
- Bird in Bush, Northumberland
- Canolfan Hermon, The Highlands
- Community Action Northumberland
- Community Heartbeat Trust
- Cornwall Rural Housing Association
- College of Agriculture, Food & Rural Enterprise, Northern Ireland
- Duke of Marlborough, Somersham, Suffolk
- East Midlands Ambulance Service
- Forest Holidays
- Friends of DalesBus, Yorkshire Dales
- Hallbankgate Hub, Cumbria
- Hastoe Housing Association
- InTouch Systems, Norfolk
- Lancashire Enterprise Partnership
- Lochcarron Community Development Company, The Highlands
- Mull & Iona Community Trust, Isle of Mull
- Nationwide Community Foundation
- NEDCare, Devon
- Nextdoor
- Northamptonshire ACRE
- Northern Fells Rural Development Group
- Northumberland Community Development Company
- Over the Bridges, Upper Coquetdale, Northumberland
- People United for Banton, North Lanarkshire
- Rural Coffee Caravan, Suffolk
- Sedlescombe Parish Council, East Sussex
- Sherston Old School CIC, Wiltshire
- South Western Housing Society
- Stow Minster, Lincolnshire
- St Tudy Community Shop, Cornwall
- The Gather, Ennerdale, Cumbria
- The Little White Bus Community Minibus, North Yorkshire
- The New Inn, Norton Lindsey, Warwickshire
- The Rural Business Group, Nottinghamshire
- Trelawnyd Community Association, Flintshire
- Upper Teesdale Agricultural Support Services, County Durham
- Wealden Wheels Community Transport, Kent
- Wereham Village Hall, Norfolk

INDEX